The BHS
Complete
Training Manual
■ FOR ■
Stage 1

The BHS
Complete
Training Manual

FOR

Stage 1

THE BRITISH HORSE SOCIETY

ISLAY AUTY FBHS

Updated and expanded by

MARGARET LININGTON-PAYNE, BHSI

KENILWORTH PRESS

Previously published under the title *The BHS Training Manual for Stage 1*, this updated and expanded edition, with the new title: *The BHS Complete Training Manual for Stage 1*, is first published in the UK in 2008 by Kenilworth Press, an imprint of Quiller Publishing Ltd

Reprinted 2009

British Library Cataloguing in Publication Data
A catalogue record for this book is available from the British Library

ISBN 978-1-905693-20-7

Layout by Kenilworth Press

Printed in Malta by Gutenberg Press

KENILWORTH PRESS
An imprint of Quiller Publishing Ltd
Wykey House, Wykey, Shrewsbury
Shropshire, SY4 1JA
tel: 01939 261616 fax: 01939 261606
e-mail: info@quillerbooks.com
website: www.kenilworthpress.com

DISCLAIMER: The authors and publishers shall have neither liability nor responsibility to any person or entity with respect to any loss or damage caused or alleged to be caused directly or indirectly by the information contained in this book. While the book is as accurate as the authors can make it, there may be errors, omissions, and inaccuracies.

Contents

Picture acknowledgements

All line drawings are by **Dianne Breeze**, with the exception of those on pages 64 (right), and 85, which are by **Carole Vincer**.

The arena diagrams on pages 120 and 121 are by **Michael J. Stevens**.

Picture sources
The author and publishers wish to acknowledge the following books as sources for some of the illustrations:

- **The BHS Manual of Equitation**, Consultant Editor Islay Auty FBHS, published by Kenilworth Press

- **The BHS Complete Manual of Stable Management**, Consultant Editor Islay Auty FBHS, published by Kenilworth Press

- **The BHS Instructors' Manual for Teaching Riding**, by Islay Auty FBHS, published by Kenilworth Press

- **Threshold Picture Guide No. 8, Field Management**, by Mary Gordon Watson, published by Kenilworth Press

- **Threshold Picture Guide No. 16, Feet and Shoes**, by Toni Webber, published by Kenilworth Press

- **The Horsemaster's Notebook**, by Mary Rose, published by Kenilworth Press

Introduction

What is the BHS Horse Knowledge and Riding Stage 1?

The four BHS Stage examinations, of which the Stage 1 is the first level, are generally taken by professional people wishing to work in the horse industry. The lower standards (primarily 1 and 2) are also used by keen amateur riders and horse owners who want to work for a valued qualification and achieve a standard of competence well recognised and respected in the horse industry. Each Stage exam includes a riding section, and a stable management section (called 'horse knowledge and care'). The two sections can be taken together on the same day, or separately. The complete qualification will not be awarded until both sections have been successfully achieved. Separate certificates are awarded for each section, and a final Stage 1 certificate.

The BHS Stage 1 Riding is a qualification which requires that the candidate is capable of riding a quiet, experienced horse or pony in an enclosed space, in walk, trot and canter. Candidates must understand the basic principles of horse care and, working under supervision, they must show some knowledge and practice of looking after a well-mannered horse in the stable and at grass.

The exam is open to members of the BHS who have reached the age of 14 years and are keen to improve their knowledge of horses and riding. Candidates holding Progressive Riding Tests 1–6 complete are eligible to have exemption from Stage 1 and can progress directly to Stage 2.

Training for the BHS Stage 1 exam is available at most BHS Approved riding schools throughout the UK, and certainly through every BHS 'Where to Train' centre. The British Horse Society runs a scheme of approval of riding schools and training centres whereby the establishments are regularly inspected on the quality and level of instruction they offer. Approved riding schools direct their teaching primarily at the leisure rider – those who ride weekly or more frequently for pleasure. Where to Train centres are specifically orientated towards clients working towards a career in the horse industry, whether as full- or part-time students. Most centres run some kind of structured training towards the

Stage examinations. This training may be on a 'one day a week' basis, it might be in a weekly evening class, or it may be by private arrangement between the instructor and the individual concerned.

A qualified BHS instructor should be able to give you guidance as to your standard and ability and how much help and training you need towards your goal of taking and passing the BHS Stage 1 exam. The more highly qualified your instructor, and especially if he or she is a BHS assessor (which means they assess Stage 1 exams), the more able he/she should be to give you sound advice about how to train for and achieve the standard to which you aspire.

Training

It is impossible to say how much training is necessary because it will depend on:

- Your initial standard.

- How much time and effort you can commit to the goal of achieving Stage 1.

- How much financial commitment you are able to make to the training and the fees for sitting the exam.

- How you respond to training and therefore how quickly you progress.

- Other variables such as family commitments, unexpected circumstances, etc.

You should feel confident about the person with whom you will be training. It is important, too, that you can work in a way that motivates you to further your own progress. There may be areas of the theory knowledge where you will need to study on your own. You may be able to work with other like-minded trainees, and this gives you the chance to gauge your progress against others working with the same aim. If you have a horse of your own at home you can practise the tasks that you will be expected to demonstrate in the exam.

How the Stage 1 is assessed

All BHS examinations are taken at specially selected BHS examination centres. All exam centres have to be Where to Train centres and are guaranteed to offer a good standard of horses to ride and facilities in which to carry out the practical aspects of the exam. The exam is run by the BHS and a panel of assessors (three or four) under the organisation of a chief assessor. The chief assessor oversees the standard and guides the team who examine the competence of the candidates.

A Stage 1 exam usually takes approximately half a day to complete and the candidates (usually a maximum of eighteen in one day) are divided into three groups. Each candidate can expect to cover a large part of the syllabus in the work he or she is asked to demonstrate.

The syllabus is divided into **compulsory** and **supporting** elements. Compulsory elements are subjects that will certainly be examined and in which the candidate must demonstrate knowledge and competence. Supporting elements are less critical, **may** be examined and provide supporting evidence of competence.

Assessors are trained and experienced in both their ability to communicate well with you, the candidate, when you are nervous and apprehensive and to assess your overall competence at the level, in spite of nerves perhaps adversely affecting your performance. The assessors will:

- Aim to be friendly and 'human', putting you at ease.

- Be clear in all the questions they ask you and in their explanation of the tasks they require you to carry out.

- Be quick to rephrase a question if they think you are not clear about what they are looking for.

- Genuinely be looking to pass you on what you can do and do know, rather than trying to find fault and fail you.

- Be trying to help you to give your best, in spite of your inevitable nerves.

In return you must:

- Know your work thoroughly and have rehearsed or practised it until it is second nature to you and will come through even if you are a little nervous.

- Believe in yourself and in your ability to pass the exam.

- Acknowledge that you will feel nervous but do not allow your nerves to swamp you so that you are unable to demonstrate your competence. Assessors never fail candidates who are up to standard, but candidates fail themselves if they allow their nerves to get the better of them.

- If you make a mistake, remember that while it may seem major to you it is probably fairly minor, and it will only be of consequence if you then allow the rest of your performance to be affected by your perception of that one mistake. You must be able to focus forward on the rest of your day even if you perceive that you have made a major error.

See also page 137 for further information on the exam day itself.

Note that you do need to register and so become a member of the BHS to be able to apply to take a Stage exam.

Working with horses – a few words of advice

If you are embarking on a career in the horse industry and are taking this exam as the first rung on the ladder to professionally recognised qualifications, it will help to consider a few important points.

Your training should instil in you **high standards** which you should strive to adhere to. Take pride in working to a high standard and always produce work that is to the best of your ability.

Good manners, communication and **discipline** are essential in dealing with horses, which can be potentially dangerous if not managed in a well-disciplined 'safe' way. Personal discipline usually develops from a well-disciplined childhood, schooldays, or perhaps, in this case, in the training environment that you have now entered.

The nature of working with horses dictates that it is a very practical 'hands on' type of work, requiring that you develop and maintain **physical fitness**. When you first start working full-time with horses you may find the work very tiring, especially if you have been used to doing only your own horse(s) at home. You will come through this early period of fatigue and every day it will get better and easier. Make sure, though, that you pace yourself and do not end up physically exhausted. Avoid 'burning the candle at both ends', eat sensibly and leave time for one or two early nights a week, particularly if you have to get up first thing in the morning. Over the first three months your stamina and physical fitness will develop quite dramatically. From the start of your career with horses, make sure that you carry heavy weights correctly, balance yourself when you carry anything awkward, and use a sack trolley or similar to move bales or heavy items if you have no one to help you.

Stage 1
Horse Knowledge and Care

Syllabus

The candidate must understand the basic principles of horse care and, working under supervision, he/she must show some knowledge and practice of looking after a well-mannered horse in the stable and at grass.

Candidates will be expected to give practical demonstrations, as well as be involved in discussion of selected tasks and topics.

IMPORTANT: Candidates are advised to check that they are working from the latest examination syllabus, as examination content and procedure are liable to alteration. Contact the BHS Examinations Office for up-to-date information regarding the syllabus.

STAGE ONE - Syllabus

Stage 1 - Horse Knowledge and Care

Candidates must be physically fit in order to carry out yard and fieldwork efficiently without undue stress and strain. They will be expected to demonstrate competent use of time. Candidates will be expected to give practical demonstrations as well as be involved in discussion of selected tasks and topics.

Unit code number S1CARE

Learning Outcomes	Element	Assessment criteria	Influence
The candidate should be able to:		*The candidate has achieved this outcome because s/he can:*	
Grooming Know how to:- Groom a horse. Put on a tail bandage.	1.1.1	Identify all items within the grooming kit	Supporting
	1.2.1	Give the uses and purpose of individual items within a grooming kit	Compulsory
	1.3.1	Show the sequence of an effective grooming procedure when brushing off / quartering	Compulsory
	1.4.1	Give the reasons for grooming	Supporting
	1.4.2	Apply safe procedures	Compulsory
	1.5.1	Show how to safely and efficiently apply a tail bandage	Compulsory
	1.5.2	Show how to safely and efficiently remove a tail bandage	Supporting
Clothing Know how to:- Put on various types of rugs including a New Zealand. Fit a roller, surcingle and cross surcingles and understand their various uses. Take off horse clothing safely.	2.1.1	Identify various stable rugs and their method of securing	Supporting
	2.1.2	Identify Turn-out rugs and their methods of securing	Compulsory
	2.2.1	Demonstrate the correct fitting of individual rugs and identify any faults	Supporting
	2.3.1	Demonstrate rugging-up appropriately with regard for safety	Compulsory
	2.3.2	Demonstrate removing rugs appropriately with regard for safety	Compulsory
Saddlery Know how to:- Put on a saddle, a numnah and a snaffle bridle (with appropriate noseband with martingale/breastplate). Check tack for safety and comfort of horse and rider. Remove tack and understand immediate aftercare. Recognise worn or ill-fitting saddlery, being aware of the dangers involved. Name parts of the saddle and bridle.	3.1.1	Identify the parts of the Saddle	Supporting
	3.1.2	Identify parts of the Bridle	Supporting
	3.1.3	Demonstrate how to put on a Martingale	Supporting
	3.1.4	Demonstrate how to put on a Hunting Breastplate	Supporting
	3.2.1	Recognise worn or damaged tack	Compulsory
	3.3.1	Discuss the consequences of worn or dirty tack	Supporting
	3.4.1	Demonstrate a safe and efficient method of tacking up	Compulsory
	3.4.2	Demonstrate a safe and efficient method of un-tacking	Compulsory
	3.5.1	Show how to fit a numnah	Compulsory
	3.6.1	Show and or discuss how to secure various types of noseband	Compulsory
	3.7.1	Show and or discuss how to clean tack	Compulsory
Handling Know how to:- Put on, fit and care for headcollars, halters and lead ropes. How and where to tie up a horse, in the stable and outside. Be practical and workmanlike.	4.1.1	Give the principles of safety when working with horses	Compulsory
	4.2.1	Show correct handling techniques	Compulsory
	4.3.1	Demonstrate how to put on a headcollar	Compulsory
	4.4.1	Tie up horses safely and efficiently	Compulsory
	4.5.1	Show efficient use of time in each task.	Compulsory
	4.6.1	Maintain a clean working environment	Compulsory

STAGE 1 SYLLABUS JANUARY 2008

Unit code number S1CARE			
Learning Outcomes	**Element**	**Assessment criteria**	**Influence**
The candidate should be able to:		*The candidate has achieved this outcome because s/he can:*	
Horse husbandry Know:- Types of Bedding. Mucking out. Bedding down. Skipping out. Setting fair. Building and maintaining a muck heap. Keeping all areas swept and tidy.	5.1.1	Give a variety of bedding materials	Supporting
	5.1.2	Give reasons for using different types of bedding	Supporting
	5.1.3	Show and or discuss how to maintain different types of bed	Supporting
	5.2.1	Demonstrate efficient, safe procedures for mucking out	Compulsory
	5.2.2	Demonstrate efficient, safe procedures for skipping out	Compulsory
	5.2.3	Demonstrate efficient, safe procedures for bedding down	Compulsory
	5.2.4	Demonstrate efficient, safe procedures for setting a bed fair	Compulsory
	5.3.1	Demonstrate safe efficient use of stable tools	Compulsory
	5.4.1	Describe how to build a muck heap	Supporting
Foot and Shoeing Know how to - Maintain the horses feet in good condition. Be able to - Recognise overgrown feet, risen clenches, worn, loose or 'sprung' shoes.	6.1.1	Pick out feet into a skip	Compulsory
	6.1.2	Wash feet	Supporting
	6.1.3	Oil hooves	Supporting
	6.2.1	Comment on the condition of the shoe in-front of you using correct terminology	Compulsory
	6.3.1	Recognise a well shod foot	Compulsory
	6.3.2	Recognise long feet	Supporting
	6.3.3	Recognise risen clenches	Supporting
	6.3.4	Recognise worn shoes	Compulsory
Anatomy and Handling Know:- The main external areas (forehand, middle, hindquarters). Basic points of the horse, their colours and markings. How to stand a horse up correctly in the stable and/or outside. How to lead and turn horses at walk and trot. How to hold a reasonably quiet horse for treatment, shoeing and clipping.	7.1.1	Identify points of the horse	Compulsory
	7.2.1	Use correct terminology when describing the horses coat colour	Compulsory
	7.2.2	Use correct terminology when describing horses markings	Compulsory
	7.3.1	Show how to hold a horse for treatment	Compulsory
	7.3.2	Show how to stand the horse up for inspection	Supporting
	7.4.1	Demonstrate safe, effective leading in hand at walk for an observer	Compulsory
	7.4.2	Demonstrate safe, effective leading in hand at trot for an observer	Supporting
	7.4.3	Demonstrate safe, correct turning of the horse when leading in hand for an observer	Compulsory
Health and Safety Know:- The importance of physical fitness in order to carry out yard work efficiently without stress and strain, use correct methods for stable tasks, lifting, moving heavy weights. How to fill, weigh and tie up a hay-net.	8.1.1	Recognise hazardous lifting situations	Compulsory
	8.1.2	Show safe lifting procedures	Compulsory
	8.1.3	Show safe carrying procedures	Compulsory
	8.2.1	Show how to fill a haynet	Supporting
	8.2.2	Show how to weigh a haynet	Supporting
	8.2.3	Show how to safely and efficiently tie up a haynet	Compulsory
	8.2.4	Recognise potential dangers when using a haynet	Supporting
Horse Health Know the signs of good health in horses and ponies recognise when they are off-colour and the importance of an immediate report.	9.1.1	State what you must look for at Morning inspections	Supporting
	9.1.2	State what you must look for at last thing at night inspections	Supporting
	9.2.1	Recognise signs of good health	Compulsory
	9.2.2	Recognise signs of ill health	Compulsory
	9.3.1	Give the reasons for reporting when a horse is unwell	Compulsory

Unit code number S1CARE			
Learning Outcomes	Element	Assessment criteria	Influence
The candidate should be able to:		The candidate has achieved this outcome because s/he can:	
Horse Behaviour Show knowledge of the horse's natural life-style, instincts, actions and reactions.	10.1.1	Outline the horses lifestyle in the wild	Supporting
	10.2.1	Describe the horses basic instincts of survival	Supporting
	10.3.1	Describe how to handle the horse in the stable	Compulsory
	10.3.2	Describe how to handle the horse in the field	Compulsory
	10.3.3	Describe how to handle the horse when ridden	Compulsory
	10.4.1	Describe signs of danger as shown in the horses expression when in the field	Supporting
	10.4.2	Describe signs of danger as shown in the horses expression when in the stable	Supporting
	10.4.3	Describe signs of danger as shown in the horses expression when ridden	Supporting
Basic Grassland Care Know:- What to look for in and around the field. Daily inspections. How to turn out a horse, how to catch him and bring him in from the field. Recognise a horse sick field.	11.1.1	Describe a "horse-sick" field	Supporting
	11.1.2	Give ways a horse sick field can be avoided/ remedied	Supporting
	11.2.1	Describe what to check each day in the field	Compulsory
	11.3.1	Describe acceptable, safe methods of turning a horse out into a field	Compulsory
	11.3.2	Describe acceptable, safe methods of bringing a horse in from a field	Compulsory
Watering & Feeding Know:- General principles and the importance of cleanliness. The various types of fodder in general use, and recognise good and bad quality. Suitable feeding of horses and ponies in light work. *Definition of 'light work'; Daily walk trot canter where the horse is not stressed.*	12.1.1	Name, Oats, Barley, Sugarbeet, Bran, Coarse mix, Nuts/Cubes, Chaff.	Compulsory
	12.1.2	Recognise good quality, Oats, Barley, Sugarbeet pulp/ cubes, Bran, Coarse mix, Nuts/Cubes, Chaff.	Supporting
	12.1.3	Recognise poor quality, Oats, Barley, Sugarbeet pulp/ cubes, Bran, Coarse mix, Nuts/Cubes, Chaff.	Supporting
	12.2.1	Recognise good quality hay	Supporting
	12.2.2	Recognise bad quality hay	Supporting
	12.2.3	Recognise acceptable quality hay	Supporting
	12.3.1	Recognise good quality haylage	Supporting
	12.3.2	Recognise bad quality haylage	Supporting
	12.4.1	Discuss the dangers of feeding poor quality fodder	Compulsory
	12.5.1	Give the rules of good feeding	Compulsory
	12.6.1	Give the rules of watering	Compulsory
	12.6.2	Know the importance of cleanliness	Supporting
	12.7.1	Discuss suitable feed for a grass kept horse and or pony in light work throughout the seasons	Compulsory
	12.7.2	Discuss suitable daily quantity of feed for a grass kept horse and or pony in light work throughout the seasons	Compulsory
	12.8.1	Discuss suitable feed for a stabled horse and or pony in light work	Compulsory
	12.8.2	Discuss suitable daily quantity of feed for a stabled horse and or in light work	Compulsory
	12.9.1	Discuss suitable methods of watering horses, at grass	Compulsory
	12.9.2	Discuss suitable methods of feeding horses, at grass	Supporting
General Knowledge Know the risks and responsibilities involved when riding or leading on the public highway. Know the correct procedures in the event of an accident. Safety Rules and Fire Precautions. Knowledge of the British Horse Society's aims.	13.1.1	Describe suitable clothes to wear when working with horses	Compulsory
	13.2.1	Describe fire precautions in the work place	Compulsory
	13.3.1	Give the correct procedure in the event of an accident to a person	Compulsory
	13.4.1	Give the safety rules for riding in a class	Supporting
	13.4.2	Give the rules and good manners involved when taking horses on the public highway	Compulsory
	13.5.1	Give the aims of the British Horse Society	Supporting

As you can see from the syllabus, the knowledge and practical ability that you require for the Stage 1 exam is very clearly disseminated into 'elements'. This is to encourage you to be systematic in your training and to ensure that your practical ability is underpinned with the necessary background knowledge.

Do not be anxious that every single 'element' as listed will be examined, or that you will fail if you do not know an answer in one specific subject. As with any examination, the syllabus requires extensive study while the examination will test a section of the overall knowledge. You can be sure, though, that the examiner will want to see that your competence in handling horses in various situations at this level is supported by sound knowledge.

Notice, too, that the syllabus contains 'compulsory' and 'supporting' elements. Compulsory elements can appear in both the practical and theory sections of your exam. The supporting elements, as the name suggests, add weight to the demonstration of competence that the compulsory elements should show. During your training and studying, remember to check regularly which areas of each subject are compulsory and which are supporting. Make quite sure that you are competent and confident about **all** the compulsory elements. Make sure that you are familiar with all the supporting elements – there should be nothing within the syllabus that you have never heard of!

The following sections show the learning outcomes, elements and assessment criteria, in line with the syllabus; for ease of studying, the subjects will be listed under the element number followed by 'what the assessor will look for'.

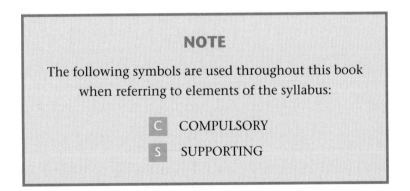

NOTE

The following symbols are used throughout this book
when referring to elements of the syllabus:

C   COMPULSORY

S   SUPPORTING

Grooming

Know how to:

Groom a horse.

Put on a tail bandage.

ELEMENT

S	**1.1.1**	Identify all items within the grooming kit.
C	**1.2.1**	Give the uses and purpose of individual items within a grooming kit.
C	**1.3.1**	Show the sequence of an effective grooming procedure when brushing off/quartering.
S	**1.4.1**	Give the reasons for grooming.
C	**1.4.2**	Apply safe procedures.
C	**1.5.1**	Show how to safely and efficiently apply a tail bandage.
S	**1.5.2**	Show how to safely and efficiently remove a tail bandage.

The grooming kit

Dandy brush: This can be used on unclipped or coarse-coated horses to remove mud and sweat. It should not be used on a horse's head, bony parts, mane or tail or on any thin-coated and/or sensitive horse as the bristles are hard and can be prickly.

Body brush: This can be used on all body parts of stabled or thin-skinned horses. It can also be used on the mane and tail. The bristles are soft and close- set, and so it should not be used on horses and ponies that live out at grass because it removes

the natural grease from the horse's coat. This grease is important for warmth and waterproofing of the coat.

Metal curry comb: This is primarily used for cleaning out the body brush. You should get into a rhythm of using the body brush on the horse for two or three strokes and then wiping the brush across the metal curry comb to remove the grease and hairs. The metal curry comb should never be used on the horse and care should be taken to ensure it is not left on the ground where a horse could tread on it and lame himself. The metal curry comb can be cleaned out by banging its edge on the floor.

Hoof pick: There are several different designs of hoof pick, but they all have the same function. Care should be taken not to drop them in the horse's bedding as the sharp end could cause injury to the horse.

Rubber curry comb: This can be used in a circular motion to remove sweat and grease from a stabled horse's coat. It can also have a massaging effect. It is very useful for removing a horse's winter coat in the spring when he is moulting.

Plastic curry comb: This is useful for horses with long coats, for removing mud and sweat. It should not be used on thin-skinned or sensitive horses.

Water brush: This brush can be used for laying a horse's mane and dampening his tail. It can also be used for washing off stable stains (marks made on a horse when he lies in his droppings).

Leather massage pad or hay wisp: These are both used to stimulate circulation and improve muscle tone. (The process is called 'banging'.) You will not be expected to demonstrate this skill in a Stage 1 examination.

Stable rubber: (a soft cloth) This can be used in conjunction

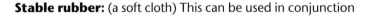

with the wisp for banging. It can also be used to remove surplus dirt and give a final polish to a stable-kept horse.

Sponges: It is essential to have at least two sponges in the grooming kit. One can be used to sponge the eyes and nose, and the other to clean the dock.

Hoof oil and brush: These are used for oiling the feet, which should not be done every day. It is best to oil the feet only on special occasions so that the foot is allowed to 'breathe'.

Sweat scraper: This is used in a motion that follows the lie of the hair, to remove excess sweat from the horse. It is also very useful for removing surplus water when the horse has had a bath.

These are the most important items of grooming kit. They should all be kept in a suitable container which should be kept tidy and cleaned out regularly.

There are other, extra items of grooming kit that you should be aware of:

Mane comb: This can be used to comb out sections of the mane and to assist when plaiting.

Tail comb: This is used for pulling the mane and tail and should not be used to brush out the tail.

Cactus cloth: This is a rough, coarse-weave cloth that can be used in a similar way to a rubber curry comb. It can sometimes come in the form of a 'mitt'.

Tail bandage: This should be put on after grooming and helps to ensure that the horse's tail is kept tidy. Tail bandages are usually 3ins (approx. 8cm) wide and made from an elasticated material.

Care of the grooming kit

All items should be kept clean. This can help to stop disease spreading.

Wash all brushes in warm water with mild detergent. Try not to get the back of the brush wet. This can loosen the bristles. When drying the brushes, give them a good shake and then place them on the ground, bristles down, to drip dry. Stable rubbers and tail bandages should be washed regularly.

Reasons for grooming

You must understand some of the reasons why we groom horses:

- It promotes health and improves circulation in the horse.

- It makes the horse feel more comfortable; and in areas where tack comes into contact with the skin, grooming ensures the horse will not be rubbed, which could lead to galls and sores.

- It improves the horse's muscle tone and so his fitness.

- It can help to build a bond between horse and owner.

- It can be used as a method to get to know the horse's usual 'lumps and bumps', thus allowing new problems to be noticed.

Grooming a stabled or grass-kept horse

Whichever type of horse, the initial process is the same. Take the horse's headcollar into the stable, close the door behind you, put the rope round the horse's neck and then put the headcollar on. Ensure that the headcollar is straight at the nose and that the mane is tidy under the headpiece at the poll. Always do the headcollar up fully – it is much safer, as it will not come undone accidentally.

Tie the horse up with a quick-release knot. If there is a choice as to where you can tie the horse, do this so that his quarters are not facing the door. It will be safer for you and the assessor coming in and out. Whenever you go in and out of the stable make sure that you close the door and put the top bolt across. (Some examination centres have chains across the door, and these should be kept fastened.) If the door is difficult to open and close, discuss this with your assessor.

This headcollar is too low on the horse's nose and not done up correctly.

A correctly fitted and fastened headcollar.

Once you have tied the horse up, the next job must be to skip out. You must keep the box skipped out. This is for economy of bedding and to make it easier for you to work. If, at any time, the horse passes droppings while you are working in the box, then take the time to skip these out as well.

Next, you should consider whether or not to take out the water bucket (if it is moveable) and the haynet. If you are grooming it is probably better to take out the water bucket as hair and dust could land in the bucket. It may be easier also to take out the haynet as the horse will then not be pulling on it as you are trying to brush his head. Some horses will, however, stand more quietly if they are able to eat. If you are in any doubt, discuss this with your assessor. If you have the same horse for all your tasks in the practical section then it may be better to take the haynet out, as you will need his attention when putting on his bridle.

Once you have got the horse and stable ready bring in your grooming kit box and put it safely at the side of the stable where the horse cannot tread on it. Also bring in a skip. A bucket with a small amount of water in will also be needed – you can leave this outside the box, or bring it in if there is room. You will only be expected to be able to quarter or brush off your horse competently. (Strapping, a full groom of the horse, is covered in Stage 2).

Quartering is the tidying up of a stable-kept horse before he does any work. Usually the rugs are folded back so the front 'two quarters' can be brushed. When this is done the front of the horse is re-covered with the rug and then it is folded forwards so the hind 'two quarters' are exposed for brushing. This ensures the horse does not get cold.

Rug folded forward to expose the horse's hindquarters.

Rug folded back to expose the horse's forequarters.

Your first task is to pick out your horse's feet. Always do this into a skip so that the dirt does not fall into the bedding (see also pages 60–63).

After picking out the feet you should brush off the horse. Use a brush that is suitable for his coat. If it is thick, use a dandy brush; if fine, or if he is clipped, then use a body brush and a metal curry comb. Traditionally, you use the hand nearest the horse to brush so that you are able to stay alert as to what his hindquarters are doing. If you find that really difficult, even though you have practised hard trying to use both hands, then as long as you are efficient and safe you will not be penalised.

Whatever brush you are using on the horse's body ensure that you are positive and efficient. Do not be aggressive, but do not, at the other end of the scale, be so timid and ineffective that your horse feels he is being tickled rather than groomed.

When you have groomed the body you can brush the legs. Unless your horse has very thick feathers it is better to use the body brush so that you do not damage the bony parts of the leg. After the legs, you can brush the mane and tail.

To brush the mane push it all over to the other side of the horse's neck and brush vigorously along the crest. Then bring the mane back over a small portion at a time and brush each section thoroughly with the body brush. You will need both hands for this so put the metal curry comb away safely in the grooming kit box.

Brushing the tail. Standing to the side of the horse will be safer for you.

To brush the tail, stand to the side of the horse, making sure that you are not trapped in a corner, and hold up the whole tail. Let a small amount of tail drop and brush it out until all the hairs are separated. Then release a little more tail and repeat the process until the whole tail has been brushed out. If the horse has a thin tail then it may be better to use your fingers rather than the body brush.

You can brush the head of the horse either before or after you have done the mane and tail. It is important to remember that there is no 'BHS way' of doing everything. There are ways of undertaking tasks safely and efficiently for you and your horse and as long as the method you use fulfils these criteria you will not be penalised.

To brush the horse's head it is better to untie the quick-release knot and leave the rope through the string. Undo the headcollar, slip it down the horse's neck and then do it up again. Take the body brush and stand facing the front of your horse. Put your right hand under his chin and over his nose to keep control, and then gently brush the head. Don't forget to brush the forelock. When you have brushed the head you can take one of the sponges and carefully sponge his eyes and nose. When you have done this you can replace the headcollar correctly.

You need now to sponge his dock. Take the other sponge and stand in the same position as you did for brushing the tail, lift the tail and wipe the area positively.

Putting on a tail bandage

You will then be asked to put on a tail bandage. Damp the tail first using the water brush and then apply the tail bandage as illustrated. The bandage should be tight enough so it does not slip down and there should be no hairs sticking out of the top. The bandage should go down to the end of the dock (as long as the horse does not have an unusually long or short dock). The ties should be tied neatly in a bow at the side of the tail (so that they do not put pressure on the horse's skin, but will not be easily rubbed undone). It is neater and safer to turn one of the overlaps of the bandage down over the ties so they are even more protected.

You will probably be asked what a tail bandage is used for and how long it should be left on.

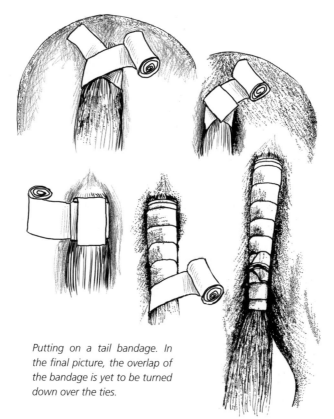

Putting on a tail bandage. In the final picture, the overlap of the bandage is yet to be turned down over the ties.

Removing a tail bandage

To remove a tail bandage, stand to the side of your horse's hindquarters, undo the tapes and grasp the top of the tail bandage with both hands. Pull smartly downwards and take the tail bandage off the tail in one movement.

If, however, the tail was plaited, you would need to unroll the tail bandage to remove it.

Uses of a tail bandage

- Shaping the tail after grooming or washing.

- Protection while travelling, whether plaited or not.

- Can be used to tie the tail up when riding in very muddy conditions, e.g. eventing.

A tail bandage should never be left on all night as it could impair the blood supply to the dock, which could lead to the hair falling out. A maximum of approximately four hours is a good guide for the appropriate length of time one can be left on.

What the assessor will look for

- You are likely to be asked to carry out a grooming procedure with a stabled or grass-kept horse. (Element 1.3.1)

- Within this procedure you will probably be asked which item of grooming kit you are using and what is the purpose of each item. (Element 1.2.1)

- You should understand the difference between quartering the horse (prior to exercise), brushing the horse off (grooming to clean up the horse after work), and a full grooming sequence (the main groom of the day, perhaps soon after exercise). (Element 1.3.1)

- You may be asked to discuss the difference between grooming a grass-kept horse and a stabled horse.

- You should be able to demonstrate competent and effective grooming of a stabled horse. You may be asked to pick out the horse's feet, use a dandy brush, and groom using a body brush and curry comb.

- You may be asked to show how to groom a mane or tail. Be clear about managing the tail and that often it is preferable only to finger through the tail to prevent damage to long tail hairs by excessive brushing.

- Be able to groom the horse's head carefully but effectively.

- Understand the need to clean and know how to deal with the eyes, mouth, nose and dock.

- You are likely to be asked why grooming is necessary, and you should be able to give health, cleanliness, comfort, safety, improving well-being, building up a relationship, and fitness among your answers. (Element 1.4.1)

- You must demonstrate safe procedures at all times. These should include awareness of the horse and how the horse is reacting to you. The horse should be safely tied up on most occasions when you are dealing with him. If the horse is not tied up but you are in the stable, then the door should be shut. Equipment should be kept tidy and organised. Always be in a safe position in relation to the position of the horse (e.g. not close to a wall when picking up hind feet).

- You will be asked to apply a tail bandage. You should be able to discuss when such a bandage might be used, how long it would be used for and how to remove it. (Elements 1.5.1 and 1.5.2)

Take every opportunity to groom as many different horses as you can, both stabled and at grass. When asked to demonstrate grooming, set about the task with a purpose, as if you really want the horse's coat to gleam. Grooming is a good experience for anyone who cares about horses and most horses thoroughly enjoy the process. For Stage 1 you must show a quiet confidence in handling well-behaved horses, and a practical ability to groom a horse effectively and apply a tail bandage.

Clothing

Know how to:

Put on various types of rug, including a New Zealand.

Fit a roller, surcingle and cross surcingles and understand their various uses.

Take off horse clothing safely.

ELEMENT

| S | **2.1.1** Identify various stable rugs and their methods of securing. |

| C | **2.1.2** Identify turn-out rugs and their methods of securing. |

| S | **2.2.1** Demonstrate the correct fitting of individual rugs and identify any faults. |

| C | **2.3.1** Demonstrate rugging-up appropriately with regard for safety. |

| C | **2.3.2** Demonstrate removing rugs appropriately with regard for safety. |

Different types of rug

New Zealand rugs

New Zealand rugs are designed for a horse to wear outdoors. They help to keep horses warm, dry and clean. There are many different designs, and innovative new materials are making New Zealand rugs lighter weight (traditional NZ rugs were heavy) and more functional. They have a waterproof outer layer, which is either canvas or man-made material, and a lining. Some designs, called 'self-righting', are much deeper than other rugs and are attached only by two breast straps and leg straps. Other types have cross-over surcingles, and older designs may have a roller-type single surcingle.

A well-fitted New Zealand rug, with gussets at the shoulder to allow for room and flexibility of movement

A New Zealand rug must fit the horse well so that the likelihood of slipping is lessened.

If a horse is living out all the time it is a good idea to have two New Zealand rugs. This means that there will be an opportunity to dry a wet rug and the horse will still be protected.

When the weather improves and the horse no longer needs to wear a New Zealand rug it may need to be re-waterproofed ready for the autumn. Always check for stitching and tears and get it repaired before storing away for the summer.

Stable/night rugs

There are even more designs of stable rug. Older rugs were made of hemp or canvas, but modern rugs are of synthetic material and are both lightweight and warm. They come in various weights and thicknesses, offering different levels of warmth. These rugs are easy to maintain and work with. The majority have cross-over surcingles and two breast straps. Some also have leg straps. Before taking a rug off you should always check to see if it has leg straps; these need to be undone and clipped back up onto their attachments before removing the rug.

Blankets

You may be asked to fit a blanket under a rug. This would give extra warmth to a horse. Rugs come in different weights and sizes and can last for many years. To fit a blanket under a rug follow the procedure shown below :

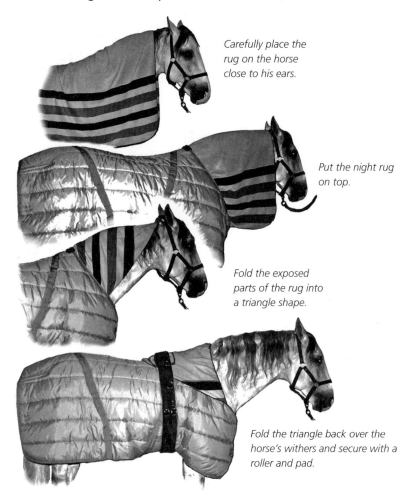

Carefully place the rug on the horse close to his ears.

Put the night rug on top.

Fold the exposed parts of the rug into a triangle shape.

Fold the triangle back over the horse's withers and secure with a roller and pad.

Sweat rugs

There are two basic types of sweat rug (some people call them anti-sweat rugs).

The old-fashioned type looks like a string vest. This rug should not be used by itself as it works by trapping air in the holes. To ensure this you need to put another rug

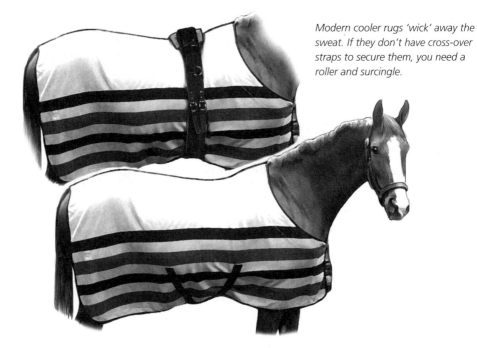

Modern cooler rugs 'wick' away the sweat. If they don't have cross-over straps to secure them, you need a roller and surcingle.

on top of it. If you do not cover it with another rug the string-vest type of rug has no real function.

The modern type of sweat rug works by 'wicking' moisture away from the horse's skin. It is very useful when travelling horses and after hard work.

Day rugs

These are made of wool, often with binding round the edges and sometimes with an embroidered name or initials on them. They are usually used on special occasions, for example when going to a show. They usually buckle at the breast and have a roller to secure them. Remember that whenever you put a roller on a horse you must put a wither pad underneath it to stop pressure on the withers.

Summer sheet

This is a rug made of thin cotton or synthetic material. It can be used to keep flies off a horse in summer. It can also be used to keep a horse clean if travelling when the weather is too hot for other rugs. As summer sheets are easy to handle and wash some people use them under stable rugs to help to keep the thicker rugs clean. As a summer sheet is a lightweight rug it will usually have a fillet string to help keep the rug in position.

A fillet string helps to keep a rug in place, especially on a windy day. Always remember to pull the tail out from under the fillet string.

A fillet string should never be so low that it could get caught over the horse's hocks.

Fitting a rug

To fit a horse well the rug must be the correct size. Rugs are sold in many different lengths, usually with 3-inch increments between one size and the next. Sometimes it can be difficult to find a rug that fits a horse – just as some people find it difficult to find a perfect fit in off-the-peg clothes.

To determine the correct rug size, measure the horse from the centre of his chest to the point of the quarters. This will give you the length required. To obtain the depth required, you will have to look at different manufacturers' styles and find the one that suits your horse.

If a rug fits well it will:

- Cover the horse from the point of his chest to the back of his dock, so that you cannot see any of his hindquarters sticking out.

- Fit snugly round the neck and not be too loose and 'gappy'.

- Overlap at the chest where the buckles are.

- Not be stretched over the shoulders.

- Not cut into the withers.

- Be deep enough to cover the barrel.

Putting on a rug

You may well be used to putting rugs on horses that you know using a throwing action. With horses you do not know this procedure should not be used as you could frighten them.

The following procedure is a safe method:

- Tie up your horse (skip out if necessary).

- If the rug has surcingles, tie them up and then fold the rug in half, inside out.

- If the rug has leg straps make sure they are hooked up. (Both these precautions will make sure that you and the horse do not get hit by metal attachments.)

- Talk to the horse and approach him on the near side.

- Place the near-side part of the front of the rug some way up the horse's neck and

APPLYING A RUG.

A folded rug, placed well up over the withers, is being secured in front.

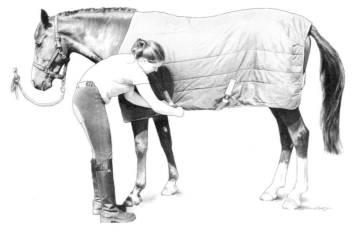

With the rug unfolded and in place, the attachments – here cross-surcingles – are fastened.

lay the offside section of the rug over his neck, so the rug is half on the horse.

- Do up the breast buckles.

- Gently pull the rug back to the correct position. (Never pull a rug forwards against the lie of the hair as this can ruffle the hair and make the horse uncomfortable.)

- Fold the rug back so it covers the horse.

- Fasten the surcingles. If there are two they will cross over. They should be tight enough so that the rug will not slip. You should be able to slide a flat hand between the horse and the straps.

- If there are leg straps, do them up as shown in the illustration below. You should be able to get the width of a hand between each strap and the horse's leg.

Rear view of leg straps interlinked.

- Finally run your hand under the rug at the withers to ensure the mane is flat on the side the mane falls.

- If the rug does not have surcingles and you have to use a roller, then the process is similar except that you must ensure there is a wither pad and the surcingle is done up tight enough to minimise the possibility of slipping.

To take off a rug

- Tie up your horse (skip out if necessary).

- Undo the breast buckles and then the surcingles or roller. (If there is a roller, take this off as soon as you have undone it.)

- Undo the leg straps and clip them back up.

(There is much discussion as to the order in which these three items are undone – as long as the method is safe for the situation then there will not be problems. As you should always start at the horse's head, it is sensible to at least undo the breast strap first. Then if there is a problem of any kind the rug will be able to fall off and not hang around the horse's neck. If you undo the leg straps first, always go to the horse's head and talk to him before approaching his bottom.)

- Fold the rug(s) back in half over the horse's hindquarters and slide them back and off the horse's back.

- The rugs can then be folded up and stored safely, ready for use.

What the assessor will look for

- You will be asked to apply rugs to a stabled horse. (Elements 2.3.1 and 2.3.2)

- The type of rug you are asked to apply may depend on the time of year and the weather conditions. You may need to make a choice of rug – say, a summer sheet for a warm, sunny day or a heavier stable rug for a colder winter's day.

- You should be familiar with the range of rugs which may be used through the year for stabled horses. Be aware of the difference in the way rugs are attached. (Element 2.1.1)

- You are likely to be asked to fit a New Zealand rug. Make sure that you have tried to see several different ways in which rugs are fitted and attached. (Element 2.1.2)

- It is likely that you will have to discuss correct rug fitting. You must show that you understand how a rug should fit around the neck, along the back (correct length) and down the body (correct depth); you should also know about the overall suitability of attachments for securing the rug safely in place.

- Throughout your application and removal of rugs, you must demonstrate safety in your handling of the horse and safe positioning of yourself in relation to the horse. Awareness is the key word. (Elements 2.3.1 and 2.3.2)

- Whilst it would be usual to remove several rugs or blankets together, be sure that all attachments have been undone so that the rugs can all be smoothly slid off the horse's hindquarters.

Horse clothing designs change nearly every year, and each type of rug updates the last for lightness, warmth, waterproof properties, etc. Your role is to try to identify the rugs you are asked to fit and describe them to the best of your ability in terms of how they fit the horse and what their role is.

If considering the general application of a rug then decide what type of rug it is and which purpose it will serve. For example, is it waterproof? Nylon quilted? Lightweight? Anti-sweat? Or a fleece-type under-rug?

You must demonstrate competence in handling rugs, putting them on and removing them efficiently, without inconveniencing the horse in any way.

Either place the rugs over the stable door as you remove them (if the stable is indoors or has an overhang over it) or remove them at once to a suitable storage area. Don't leave rugs on the stable floor where they can pick up bedding or get damp, or where some horses may chew them.

Saddlery

Know how to:

Put on a saddle, a numnah, and a snaffle bridle (with appropriate noseband with martingale/breastplate).

Check tack for safety and comfort of horse and rider.

Remove tack and understand immediate aftercare.

Recognise worn or ill-fitting saddlery, being aware of the dangers involved.

Name parts of the saddle and bridle.

ELEMENT

S	**3.1.1**	Identify the parts of the saddle.
S	**3.1.2**	Identify the parts of the bridle.
S	**3.1.3**	Demonstrate how to put on a martingale.
S	**3.1.4**	Demonstrate how to put on a hunting breastplate.
C	**3.2.1**	Recognise worn or damaged tack.
S	**3.3.1**	Discuss the consequences of worn or dirty tack.
C	**3.4.1**	Demonstrate a safe and efficient method of tacking up.
C	**3.4.2**	Demonstrate a safe and efficient method of untacking.
C	**3.5.1**	Show how to fit a numnah.
C	**3.6.1**	Show and/or discuss how to secure various types of noseband.
C	**3.7.1**	Show and/or discuss how to clean tack.

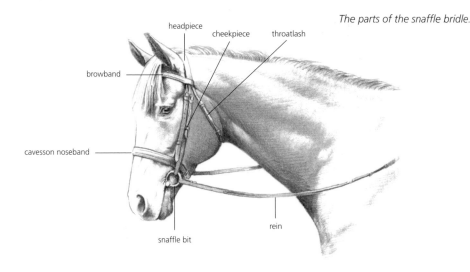

The parts of the snaffle bridle.

headpiece

cheekpiece   throatlash

browband

cavesson noseband

rein

snaffle bit

You will be asked to tack up a horse with its own saddle and bridle. You will not be expected to fit the tack but should be able to recognise whether or not the tack is comfortable for the horse and is safe for both horse and rider.

Preparing to tack up

To tack up a horse safely, firstly tie the horse up and skip out if necessary. Once the horse is tied up, you can collect the tack, and if there is no possibility of the horse knocking the saddle off the door you can rest the saddle on the stable door. If this is not possible then leave the saddle outside the stable until you are ready to put it on. If at any time you need to put the saddle on the floor then make sure it is out of harm's way. Always place the saddle pommel down and with the cantle leaning against the wall. Put the girth in between the cantle and the wall so that the leather does not get marked.

When putting a saddle on the ground, lean the cantle against a wall with the girth so placed to protect it.

The parts of the saddle.

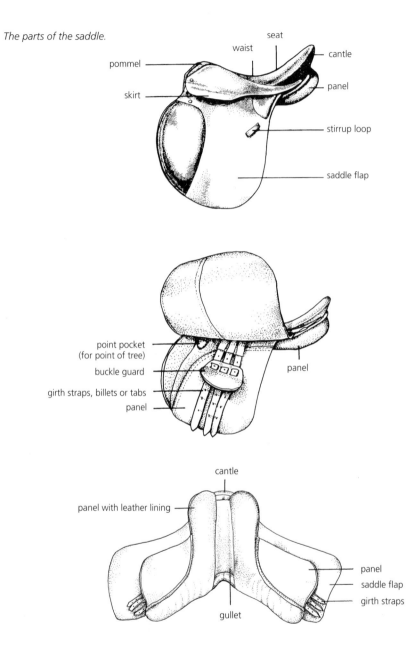

seat

waist

pommel

cantle

skirt

panel

stirrup loop

saddle flap

point pocket
(for point of tree)

buckle guard

girth straps, billets or tabs

panel

panel

cantle

panel with leather lining

panel

saddle flap

girth straps

gullet

It does not matter if you put the saddle or the bridle on first, but if you have to fit a martingale or breastplate it is better to put the bridle on first so that you do not have to undo the girth once it is done up.

Putting on a bridle

Check that the bridle is ready to be put on with the noseband undone.

There are several different types of noseband. You will probably have one of the following to put on: a cavesson, a flash, a drop or a grakle.

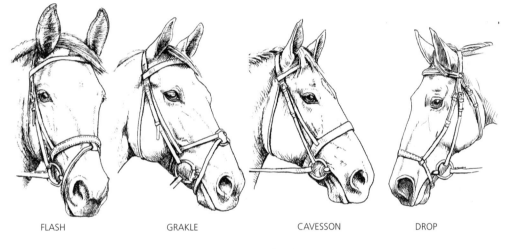

FLASH   GRAKLE   CAVESSON   DROP

Various nosebands.

- Hold the bridle up to the side of the horse's head to check that it is the correct size.

- Undo the lead rope and leave it through the string loop.

- Undo the headcollar and slip it round the horse's neck and do it up again.

- Put the reins over the horse's ears and hold the bridle in your left hand.

- If you want, now you have control of the horse, you can take the headcollar from round his neck and buckle it up through the tie ring. Never leave a headcollar on the floor – you or the horse could get a foot caught in it.

- Face forwards and put your right hand under the horse's head and round the offside so that you can hold the bridle by the cheek pieces in this hand.

Putting on a bridle. By passing your right hand under his chin and over his face you have more control of the horse.

As well as holding and lifting the bridle, the right hand can also (if necessary) put pressure on the front of his face to stop him putting his head up.

- Put the bit in your left hand and lift it to his mouth. He should open his mouth. Then your right hand can lift the bridle so that the bit lifts into his mouth. If he does not open his mouth then your left thumb can safely be put into his mouth at the corner of his lips – he has no teeth here and this is where the bit lies. Putting your thumb into the corner of his mouth will automatically cause him to open his mouth, and you can then lift the bridle with your right hand.

- You can then gently lift the headpiece into place by folding the horse's ears through the leather.

- Make sure you pull the forelock out from under the browband and that you run your fingers under the headpiece to tidy the mane at the poll. It is uncomfortable for the horse to be left without his mane being tidied up.

- If you have not already taken the headcollar from around the horse's neck, you can do this now. Remember to buckle the headcollar through the tie ring and not leave it dragging on the floor.

- If the horse is going to be left in the stable it is safest to twist the reins a few times and put one of the reins up through the throatlash as you do this up. The throatlash should be done up loosely enough to allow a flat hand's width between it and the horse's jaw bone. The noseband should be done up tightly enough that you can get at least one finger between the leather and the front of the horse's nose. There is a great deal of discussion as to how tight a noseband should or should not be and owners will vary as to how tight or loosely they like it done up.

- There are also different types of noseband that you might encounter. If you have to do up a noseband with a flash strap make sure that the buckle is nowhere near the horse's lips as this could rub and make him sore.

- Once you have successfully put on the bridle check that everything is level and straight. The noseband and browband should not be lopsided on the horse's head.

- You can then put the headcollar on over the bridle (making sure that the headcollar is not too low on the nose) and re-tie the quick-release knot.

Putting on a martingale

You may well have a running martingale to put on with the bridle. The martingale will probably already be attached to the reins and there is no necessity to take it off the reins to put it on. Check that the martingale strap has its buckle on the near side and then put the martingale neck strap over the horse's head at the same time as you put the reins over his head. You can still twist the reins and put one rein through the throatlash. You will just need to remember to put the loop of the martingale through the girth when you put on the saddle. Always check that the loop is in the middle of the front legs so that it does not rub on a leg.

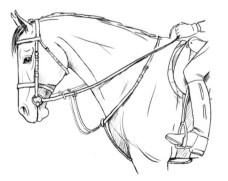

Correctly fitted running martingale. It will have no action when the horse's head is in the correct position.

This running martingale is far too short and is continually putting pressure on the horse's mouth through the reins.

A running martingale is designed to stop a horse putting his head up beyond the point of control.

In Stage 1 you are not expected to discuss the fitting of tack, but you need to know and understand what is safe and comfortable for the horse. The martingale straps should not put pressure on the reins when the horse is standing still. The martingale should only come into action when the horse tries to throw his head up high, beyond the point of control.

There should always be rubber martingale stops on the reins to ensure that the martingale rings do not slip down the reins towards the bit and catch on the buckles or billets.

If the running martingale is not already attached to the reins then once both the bridle and the martingale are on the horse you need to undo the reins at the buckle end and hold up the martingale ring for each rein so that it is not twisted and will slide up and down the rein with ease. Then thread the rein through the ring and repeat with the other ring. You can then re-buckle the reins.

You must be able to recognise:

■ Whether the bridle pinches the horse at the base of his ears.

■ Whether the browband is too loose or too tight.

■ If the bit is too high or too low in the horse's mouth.

■ If the bridle suits the horse – is the leather wide enough for his head or is it too wide? (A horse with a fine head looks unattractive with a very thick leather bridle.)

■ Whether the bridle is in good condition – is it supple and clean or does the leather need a good oiling? Is the bridle old, but in good condition? Is all the stitching safe? You may be asked if you feel it is safe to hack the horse out in the bridle he is wearing. Be practical – if the bridle is old and in good condition, and the horse is comfortable in it, then there will be nothing wrong with using it to hack out in. If the leather is cracked and shows signs of rotting stitching or worn leather then it may well not be safe. Always check where leather and metal meet – this is an area of wear and tear and so a potential weak spot.

Putting on the saddle

Once you have put on the bridle you should put the saddle on as soon as possible to complete the task. You will be asked to put a numnah or saddlecloth on with the saddle. You will probably have a general-purpose saddle to put on, but have a look at the saddle to see what type it is.

Different types of saddle.

GENERAL PURPOSE

DRESSAGE

JUMPING

- Put the numnah on the horse's back a little further forward than you want it and make sure you tidy the mane at the withers. Make sure the numnah is equal on both sides of the horse.

- If the girth is attached to the saddle on the offside then make sure you lay it over the seat of the saddle or put it up through the offside stirrup so that it will not flap and bang the horse's legs. Place the saddle onto the numnah, again a little further forward than the final position, and then pull the numnah up into the gullet of the saddle. You can then gently push the saddle at the pommel with the heel of your palm and it will slide into the correct place. By using the heel of your palm it will ensure that you are not just pushing back – you are pushing down as well. Make sure that you can see the numnah all the way round the saddle, and that it is still pulled up high into the gullet.

- You can now attach the numnah to the saddle by whatever means there are. Different types of numnahs have differing means of attachment, but generally there is some form of connection that will attach to the girth straps and a loop for the girth to go through. It is important to attach these on both sides so that the numnah does not slip back.

- If the numnah is already attached to the saddle then it is not necessary to undo it and put it on separately. It is important, however, to make sure that the numnah is correct under the saddle, i.e. it is well up into the gullet and is level on both sides. If you think it is easier to ensure this by putting them on separately then do this, but you need to be practical and efficient.

- Once you have checked that the numnah is safe you can go to the offside and put down the girth, and attach the numnah if not already done. Place the girth down gently so it does not knock the horse's leg.

- Always check that the girth is correctly connected on the first and third buckle straps and that the buckle guard is pulled down over the straps. The buckles should be done up on the first and third straps because of the way they are attached to the saddle. If you look at the top of the straps you will see they are attached to the saddle tree by webbing. The first strap is attached by one piece of webbing and the second and third together by another piece. If one of the pieces of webbing should break you want each girth strap to be attached via a different piece of webbing to ensure that your girth is still done up.

- Come back to the near side and reach under the horse's belly for the girth. If you have a martingale then remember to put the girth through the loop. Put the girth

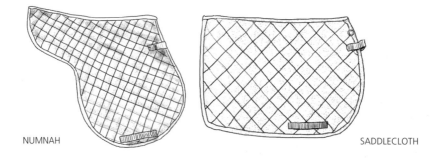

NUMNAH   SADDLECLOTH through the numnah loop and then do it up on the first and third girth straps tightly enough so that the saddle will not slip. Pull the buckle guard down over the buckles and then wait for the assessor to come and talk to you. If it is a cold day put a rug over the horse.

Putting on a hunting breastplate

Instead of a running martingale you might be asked to put on a hunting breastplate. This is designed to stop a saddle slipping backwards while the horse is in work.

■ If you have to put one of these on then put it over the horse's head before or after putting on the bridle, but before the saddle. If you put the saddle on and do up the girth first then you will have to undo the girth again to put the breastplate on. This will take extra time and make you look inefficient. The girth needs to be passed through the breastplate loop in exactly the same way as the martingale. Once the girth is done up you need to check that the leather is in the middle of the horse's front legs and not pulled up close to one leg or the other (the same as for a martingale).

■ Once the girth is attached and the saddle is secure you can affix the two small leather straps to the D rings of the saddle. If the saddle has two D rings on each side you should use the Ds that are attached directly to the tree and not those attached to the saddle by a small piece of leather. The Ds attached directly to the saddle are stronger and less likely to break under pressure.

■ You should be able to get approximately one hand's width between the leather and the horse round his neck and chest area, and the straps attached to the saddle should be tight enough to come into action should the saddle start to slightly move backwards. It is important that there is not a big loop under the horse's belly as potentially he could catch a foot in it.

Discussing the task with the assessor

When the assessor comes to talk to you, take off the rug and the headcollar so that you can show the tasks you have done and talk about the tack. Do not be afraid to touch the tack as you are talking about it, but always be aware of your own and the horse's safety.

When talking about the saddle, as for the bridle, say what you feel about the quality of the tack, how safe it is and how comfortable for the horse. If the saddle is old and in good condition and appears safe and comfortable for the horse then there will be no problem. Talk about the fit of the numnah relative to the horse and the saddle. Check the stirrup leather stitching for safety and make sure the stirrups have stirrup treads in them. Hopefully you will not have nickel stirrup irons (as these are infrequently found these days) but if you do you should point out that nickel is not as safe as stainless steel because it bends and breaks more easily. It is easy to tell the difference between nickel and stainless steel – nickel is a dull, almost yellowy colour, whereas stainless steel is shiny and silver.

Untacking

Once you have discussed the tack you will be asked to untack. Remember that this is still part of the exam and must be done safely and efficiently. It is better to take off the saddle first and it is essential to be done first if you have a martingale on.

- If you have a breastplate on, undo the attachments at the front of the saddle first. Then undo the girth (on the near side) and put it down gently, unthreading the martingale loop – do not just let it drop and bang on the horse's leg. Take hold of the saddle and numnah at the pommel and cantle and slide it back and up a little way, lifting it onto your right arm. You can then reach for the girth with your left arm.

- Put the saddle on the door or safely on the floor and move the horse away, towards the tying up point.

- There are several ways you can take off the bridle and end up with a headcollar on the horse and, again, as long as you do it safely and carefully it does not matter how you go about it. One way is to untie the headcollar and place it over your arm ready to use. Undo the noseband strap(s) and the throatlash. (Try to remember that whenever you are 'doing something up' on a horse start from the top down and when undoing items go from the bottom up.) You could then put the headcollar rope over the horse's neck (still keeping the headcollar on your arm). Stand and face forwards on the near side, by the horse's head, and put your right hand under the horse's head and reach for the bridle on the offside, at the point where the browband meets the headpiece. With your left hand hold the same place on the near side. Lift the bridle gently over the horse's ears and wait for him to open his mouth to let go of the bit. Do not drag the bit from his mouth

– if you hear the bit bang against his teeth then you know you have been too quick and he has been caused pain. This is an easy way to start a horse rushing and throwing his head to try and get the bridle off. Put the bridle on your other shoulder and put on the headcollar. Always remember to do up the headcollar properly through the buckle. Now you can slip the reins over the horse's head and tie him up with a quick-release knot.

Cleaning tack

You will also be asked about cleaning tack. Tack should be 'wiped over' after every use. For the bridle this involves taking all the straps from their keepers and wiping the leather with a sponge that is dampened with warm water. This will remove the dirt. You should then take saddle soap and a cloth (or a second sponge) and, without making the soap too wet, dampen it and then rub the cloth or sponge into the soap. You can then rub this cloth over the leather thus passing the soap onto the bridle. You will have to frequently rub the cloth into the saddle soap to ensure you have enough soap to pass onto the leather. You should not get the soap so wet that it lathers up. You need to do this to all the leather of the bridle. It is easier to do it if you hang the bridle on a bridle hook. If you have not already done so straight after riding you should wash the bit in clean water to remove any dirt. The saddle is 'wiped over' in the same way, making sure you soap all the undersides of the leather. You need to take the numnah off first, and any mud can be washed from the stirrups with warm water.

Strip clean

This should be undertaken once a week. The tack is taken apart (stripped down) and thoroughly cleaned.

- All parts of the bridle are undone and each piece is cleaned as above by first washing it with warm water (not getting it too wet) and then soaping. Buckles can be cleaned with metal polish and buffed up with a cloth. A major reason for doing this (as well as to keep the tack supple and in good condition) is to check all the stitching and leather for wear and tear. The bridle can then be re-assembled.

- The saddle should have the stirrups, buckle guards, girth and numnah removed. The girth (if synthetic) and numnah should be washed and the rest of the saddle cleaned in the usual way, paying particular attention to the undersides of all the leather. Never put too much soap on the seat of the saddle as this can ruin a rider's jodhpurs. The stirrup treads should be removed so they can be washed, and the stirrups cleaned and polished. The saddle can then be re-assembled.

- Occasionally tack will need to be oiled and 'fed' with leather dressing. This could be about every eight weeks, but the feel of the tack will tell you when this is needed – it will start to feel hard and no longer pliable.

- If you have very wet and/or muddy tack, rinse the mud off, allow the tack to dry naturally and then oil it.

- You may come across a synthetic saddle in your exam. To clean this you need to wipe it over with a damp cloth and then use a cleaning product specifically designed for synthetic tack. The saddle needs to be checked in the same way for safety and any problems should be brought to the attention of the senior person on the yard.

What the assessor will look for

- You will be asked to put on a snaffle bridle and saddle and then remove them again. Your procedure for doing this should demonstrate safety and awareness of the horse and yourself. (Elements 3.4.1. and 3.4.2)

- The tack should belong to the horse, in which case it should fit him. However, you should be capable of recognising that the overall appearance of the tack on the horse is comfortable and looks correct for the horse.

- Be able to consider the overall appearance of the bridle. When discussing the bridle with the assessor make sure that you have removed the headcollar if the horse was tied up before the assessor arrived. It is impossible to clearly discuss a bridle if there is a headcollar over it.

- You will probably be asked to name the parts of the saddle and bridle. (Elements 3.1.1.and 3.1.2)

- You should be able to recognise the condition of supple, well-maintained tack, and to describe tack that is neglected, cracking and dry even if the latter is not in front of you. (Element 3.2.1)

- Be able to talk about the danger and discomfort to horse and rider of using tack that is in poor condition or repair. (Element 3.3.1)

- Your application of the saddle is likely to include the use of a numnah. (Element 3.5.1) Try to familiarise yourself with different types of numnah and ensure that you can attach them to the saddle or girth to keep them in place in use. Ensure that the numnah fits well under the saddle and allows freedom over the wither.

- You will be asked to put on a hunting breastplate and/or a martingale. (Elements 3.1.3 and 3.1.4) The martingale will usually be a 'running' type, and you should check that there are 'stops' on the reins for safety. Be aware of why these pieces of equipment are used and make sure you have practised well with both.

- You may be asked to describe various different types of noseband and how these differ in the way they are applied to the horse. (Element 3.6.1) The bridle will carry one type of noseband and this will be discussed when you apply the bridle. Different nosebands may be on display for you to handle and identify.

- You may be asked to demonstrate how to clean tack, but it is more likely that you will be questioned on the method for cleaning tack. You may be asked how frequently you would clean tack and what to do with it if it was wet or muddy. (Element 3.7.1)

Your handling of the horse should demonstrate confidence and show familiarity with tacking up. You must also be able to complete the tasks in a reasonable timescale.

Handling

Know how to:

Put on, fit and care for headcollars, halters and lead ropes.

How and where to tie up a horse, in the stable and outside.

Be practical and workmanlike.

ELEMENT

| C | **4.1.1** Give the principles of safety when working with horses.
| C | **4.2.1** Show correct handling techniques.
| C | **4.3.1** Demonstrate how to put on a headcollar.
| C | **4.4.1** Tie up horses safely and efficiently.
| C | **4.5.1** Show efficient use of time in each task.
| C | **4.6.1** Maintain a clean working environment.

When putting on a headcollar, always make sure that the horse is comfortable. The mane at the poll should be tidied by running your hand under the leather the way the mane naturally drops, and the noseband should be approximately two fingers' distance down from the bottom of the protruding cheekbone.

Always do the headcollar up completely – put the end through the bottom of the buckle to ensure it is safely done up and there is no possibility of it coming undone accidentally.

What the assessor will look for

- **Always** awareness – awareness of how the horse is interacting with you around him, and awareness of your actions in relation to him. (Element 4.1.1) This

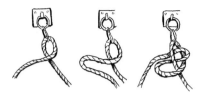

One way to tie a quick-release knot.

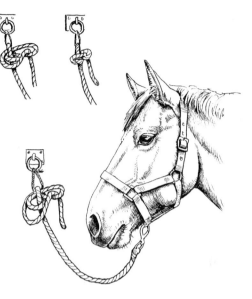

element will cover your overall confidence and competence and relates to your whole manner throughout the practical part of the exam. (Element 4.2.1)

- You must show quiet confidence in your approach to any horse (horses you may not know or have handled before).

- Be able to place the headcollar on the horse and secure it firmly. (Element 4.3.1)

- Tie the horse up with a quick-release knot (see illustration above). Preferably tie the rope through a thin piece of binder twine and not directly to the ring. If there is no twine on the ring then ask for some and state your reason for being unhappy to tie the horse directly to the ring – i.e. in case the horse pulled back and injured himself. (Element 4.4.1)

- You may be asked to discuss where it is safe to tie up horses. In stables it would usually be considered safe to leave a horse tied up in his own stable with the door shut. If the horse is tied outside then other considerations might be taken into account, e.g. the weather, or outside distractions such as other horses, noises or frightening disturbances. It would be considered a sensible precaution not to leave an unsupervised horse tied up outside.

- Safe handling involves competence and awareness – both of which should be demonstrated in your exam.

- With competence and confidence come economy in time used for tasks. As you become more proficient, all your tasks will take you less time and you therefore develop efficiency.

The assessors may not ask you anything about this section, but will be assessing your ability during the task you are undertaking. You should always appear confident when working around horses. Do not be loud, make quick movements or take the horses for granted. The horses at the exam centre may not behave like the ones you know at home, so pay particular attention to your own and the horse's safety.

Do talk to the horse before entering his box, but do not spend time 'petting' it. Always remember to approach the shoulder of the horse before going to the back, and try not to walk behind the horse. Do not get caught between the horse and a wall; be prepared to walk around the box.

It is vitally important that you come across as efficient and workmanlike. These are industry-credible qualifications and even if you are taking them purely to assess your own abilities, you must work to a standard that would be acceptable to an employer.

Horse Husbandry

Know:

Types of bedding.

Mucking out.

Bedding down.

Skipping out.

Setting fair.

Building and maintaining a muck heap.

Keeping all areas swept and tidy.

ELEMENT

S	**5.1.1** Give a variety of bedding materials.
S	**5.1.2** Give reasons for using different types of bedding.
S	**5.1.3** Show and/or discuss how to maintain different types of bed.
C	**5.2.1** Demonstrate efficient, safe procedures for mucking out.
C	**5.2.2** Demonstrate efficient, safe procedures for skipping out.
C	**5.2.3** Demonstrate efficient, safe procedures for bedding down.
C	**5.2.4** Demonstrate efficient, safe procedures for setting a bed fair.
C	**5.3.1** Demonstrate safe, efficient use of stable tools.
S	**5.4.1** Describe how to build a muck heap.

Bedding

There are numerous different types of bedding, with new brands coming on the market regularly.

Straw

There are three types of straw: oat, barley and wheat.

Wheat straw used to be the cheapest form of bedding but over the last few years it has become more expensive and some farmers no longer make the small bales that make it easy to handle and store. It makes an attractive, warm bed and is still used in many yards.

Barley straw is usually longer, of better quality and a brighter colour than wheat straw. Modern combining methods have removed the awns which used to irritate the horse's skin. Barley straw can be eaten to excess and so cause problems.

Oat straw is often used as a foodstuff so is more expensive than the other two. It is highly palatable and so eaten in excess if used as bedding.

All straw is likely to be eaten by the horse. There will be fungal spores in the straw and this can cause respiratory problems. A competition horse could have his fitness compromised if he eats too much bedding. Sprinkling the bed with non-toxic disinfectant can stop the horse from eating it.

Straw manure is easily disposed of. Well-rotted horse-straw manure is a gardener's favourite.

Wherever straw is stored there is a potential fire risk, so fire regulations must be strictly enforced.

Shavings

Shavings usually come in bales of various sizes and are of varying quality. Some are dust-extracted, which improves their quality. Shavings provide a spore-free bed that will not be eaten by the horse. If the bed is regularly skipped out it is relatively easy to keep it clean and tidy. Baled shavings are easy to store and transport. Some wood mills allow bulk collection of shavings, which can be very cheap. These may, however, be contaminated with pieces of wood and be of poorer quality. There is a specially designed fork for use with shavings, and it makes mucking out easier.

A shavings bed is not as warm as a straw bed because there is no trapped air. Shavings can be messy on the yard. They can also get into horses' tails and clothing and cannot be used for horses with open wounds. Shavings manure can also be difficult to dispose of.

Shredded paper

Shredded newspaper or office waste can be bought in bales. Some bigger yards purchase their own shredder and collect paper from clients and friends to shred and use. Shredded paper is totally dust free and ideal for horses with respiratory problems. Because it is in bales it is also easy to store. It can be heavy and difficult to work with because it is highly absorbent. It does need careful management, and it may be difficult to keep the yard tidy as the dry paper strips are easily blown across the yard. The ink from newsprint can stain the coat of grey horses, and some horses with white legs can become allergic to it. It may be difficult to dispose of, although it does eventually break down into good manure.

Shredded cardboard

Most of the points relevant to paper apply to shredded cardboard. Because it is thicker, cardboard takes longer to break down and does not form such a comfortable bed. It does not absorb moisture as quickly and can be difficult to work with.

Hemp-based bedding

There are several different forms of hemp-based bedding. Hemp is a natural fibre derived from the flax plant. It is highly absorbent, dust free and unpalatable. It does become very heavy to work with, but if well maintained can be quite economical, although the initial outlay per bale can be more than shavings.

Peat moss

This used to be an excellent, although expensive, bedding, but now for ethical, environmental reasons it should not be used.

Rubber matting

Rubber matting is currently a very popular form of floor covering for horses. It should not be used by itself. Although it can cut down hugely on the amount of bedding used on top of it, there should always be a covering of some other bedding (shavings or a hemp-based bedding are the best) to help absorb the urine. It is easy to muck out, but must be very carefully maintained otherwise the box can become very smelly. A box with rubber matting in must have first-class drainage to prevent urine pooling and not draining away. Using rubber matting and a sprinkling of bedding on top can cut down hugely on the amount of waste and consequently make the disposal of manure easier.

Mucking out

Depending on the type of bedding you are working with the process will vary a little, but the basic procedure is similar:

1. Collect the tools you need: four-pronged fork (shavings fork for non-straw beds), shovel, broom, wheelbarrow, skip. Some people prefer to work a straw bed with a two-pronged fork.

2. If possible, remove the horse from the box. This is safer, makes the task easier for you and means there will be no spores for the horse to breathe in.

3. Skip out any visible droppings. If it is a straw bed, place the skip on its side on the floor behind the pile of droppings you wish to remove. Rest the skip between your feet, take hold of the straw around

Skipping out a straw bed.

the droppings and flick the droppings into the skip. This is a quick and easy way of skipping out and saves on straw. If you have a shavings or hemp-type bed then it may be easier to put on a pair of rubber gloves and pick up the droppings. Put all the droppings into the wheelbarrow.

4. Next you need to sort out the bedding, moving all the clean bedding to one side. With a straw bed a two-pronged fork makes it easy to lift the bed a small amount and throw it to one side of the box. Make a pile of all the clean straw on one side of the box. Try to save as much bedding as possible, leaving only the very soiled bedding to be removed.

5. Now you need to remove the soiled bedding into the wheelbarrow. With a straw bed you should use a four-pronged fork. Stack the wheelbarrow by building it up and spreading out the corners. You will be able to put far more on the barrow rather than just having a pile in the middle of the barrow.

6. Sweep the floor with the broom and remove the sweepings into the barrow using the shovel.

7. Put the bedding back down. This should be done by lifting the bedding and 'throwing' it into position rather than dragging it into place. Some yards put down a 'day bed', which has just a small amount of bedding, and leave putting down the full bed until the evening. Other yards put down the complete bed and banks straight after mucking out. Banks are useful: they make the bed warmer, more comfortable and safer for the horse. Bedding from the banks can be used in

You will get more in the barrow if you stack the barrow carefully, spreading the muck into the corners.

place of the bedding that has been taken out and then new bedding can be added to the banks. To test if you have enough bedding on the floor of the box turn the fork upside down and pat it down on the bed. If you cannot feel the floor then there is sufficient bedding.

You should practise using the tools. If you have long-handled tools one hand should be at the end of the tool. This will mean you will not bend your spine too much and, if the horse is still in the box, you will not accidentally prod the horse. When you have finished using the tools they should be cleaned and put away safely.

Skipping out

This should be done regularly throughout the day. Every time you go into a horse's box get into the habit of tying him up and skipping him out. This will mean that the box will be kept tidy and it will be very economical with bedding use. In an exam you will need to keep the boxes you are working in skipped out. Practise the technique described above to become quick and efficient.

Setting a bed fair

This term refers to making the bed neat and tidy. This is most often done at the end of the day. The bed is tidied, the banks re-arranged if necessary, and the area in front of the doorway swept.

Building a muck heap

A muck heap should receive daily care. There are various ways it can be maintained and this depends on the preference of the yard. The basic principles are that the sides need to be kept vertical and the corners square. The muck heap should be well trodden down so that anaerobic bacteria can break down the manure. Some yards have three muck heaps: one that is being built, one that is breaking down, and one that is ready to be taken away. Other yards 'step' their muck heap, while some contract out their muck removal and have a large mesh container into which the muck is tipped and the container is removed when it is full. Whichever method is used, the muck heap and surrounding area must be kept tidy – a well-run establishment will always take good care of its muck area.

What the assessor will look for

- You should be familiar with most common forms of bedding, e.g. straw, shavings, paper, sawdust, rubber matting (with a reduced amount of some other bedding). (Element 5.1.1)

- You should be able to discuss why different types of bedding are used. This may be due to availability, cost, ease of disposal, personal choice or commodity that is best for a particular horse. (Element 5.1.2)

- You will be expected to discuss how to maintain some of the bedding types you have named. You should be familiar with what you use 'at home', and in addition try to be competent with at least one other type of bedding.

- You may be asked to muck out a complete stable, or you may be involved in this as a group task. In every case the procedure for organising the task and then completing it is of importance. (Element 5.2.1)

- You may be asked to bed down a stable. (Element 5.2.3)

- Be able to demonstrate the difference between mucking out the box and skipping out (removal of droppings and tidying the bed). Be clear about how to set the bed fair. You may be asked to show this. (Elements 5.2.2 and 5.2.4)

- You should demonstrate competence in handling tools for use in the stable yard including awareness of safe management and storage of tools. (Element 5.3.1)

- You may be asked how to build a muck heap, or you may be taken to look at the exam centre's muck heap and asked to comment on it. You should be conversant with the tidy building and maintenance of a muck heap and its relevance to good yard management. (Element 5.4.1)

As a member of a team in a stable yard, everyone has joint responsibility for keeping tools and equipment safely stored and managed while in use. Wheelbarrows and forks can be dangerous to horses and humans in the wrong circumstances. A tidy, well-kept yard reflects the efficiency of those who work in the establishment.

The Foot and Shoeing

Know how to:

Maintain the horse's feet in good condition.

Be able to recognise overgrown feet, risen clenches, worn, loose or 'sprung' shoes.

ELEMENT

C	**6.1.1** Pick out feet into a skip.
S	**6.1.2** Wash feet.
S	**6.1.3** Oil hooves.
C	**6.2.1** Comment on the condition of the shoe in front of you, using correct terminology.
C	**6.3.1** Recognise a well-shod foot.
S	**6.3.2** Recognise long feet.
S	**6.3.3** Recognise risen clenches.
C	**6.3.4** Recognise worn shoes.

Picking out a horse's feet

- As usual, you should tie up the horse. Find your hoof pick and a skip.

- Most horses are used to having their near fore foot picked up first. Talk to the horse as you approach him. Facing his quarters, stand close to his shoulder. Put the skip in such a position that it will catch the contents of the foot as you pick it out, and have the hoof pick in your right hand. Stroke his shoulder with your left hand and continue to run your hand down the back of his leg. When you reach the fetlock he may automatically pick up his foot and you can then hold the leg around the pastern. If he does not pick up his foot, then squeeze the fetlock. If this does not do the trick then squeeze the fetlock again and gently pull upwards. The easiest place to hold the foot is at the bottom of the pastern near to the coronary band.

- Now with the hoof pick: start at the heel and take the hoof pick down one side of the frog towards the toe. Always work from heel to toe, and if you dig into the mud it should flick it out of the hoof and into the skip. Next run the pick down the other side of the frog with the same movement. Use the pick to rake out any other mud or debris, but always remember to go from heel to toe. The frog is sensitive and if you dig the pointed part of the pick into it too sharply you can lame your horse. However, you will not lame your horse by just touching the frog, so do not be afraid if you do come into contact with it. Try to put the foot down gently; do not let it drop suddenly to the floor.

- Next move on to the near hind leg. Place the skip a little way behind the hind foot and keep the hoof pick in your right hand. Gently pat your horse on his quarters and run your hand down the outer side of his hind leg until you reach the hock. Then transfer your hand to the inner side of his hind leg and continue down, repeating the same process as for the front foot.

- You then need to go round the front of the horse, change over hands and repeat the process.

- If your horse is used to it, and you pick both front/hind feet from the same side, you would do the near fore first and then the off fore. If a horse is not used to having both feet picked out on the same side then he may become confused, so in an exam it may be better to pick out the feet from both sides.

Washing the horse's feet

You will probably not be asked to wash a horse's feet. However, if you do not perform the process you will be asked to talk about it. To wash the feet you need a bucket of water and a water brush. You need to make sure your horse is happy about the process. Make sure the brush is wet and then use it to firstly wash away any mud on the outside of the hoof and then the sole and frog. It is important to make sure you dry the heels afterwards with a towel because heels that are left wet are prone to cracking. If the feet are very muddy and the horse is happy about it you can use a hosepipe to get the worst of the mud off and then employ the water brush to finish off the job. If a horse's feet are washed regularly it is sensible to put Vaseline in the heels to help prevent cracking.

What the assessor will look for

You should already be aware that care of the horse's feet on a daily basis is one of the most essential areas of good horse management. The old saying, 'no foot, no horse' is a very relevant statement, which has been passed down through generations because of its truth.

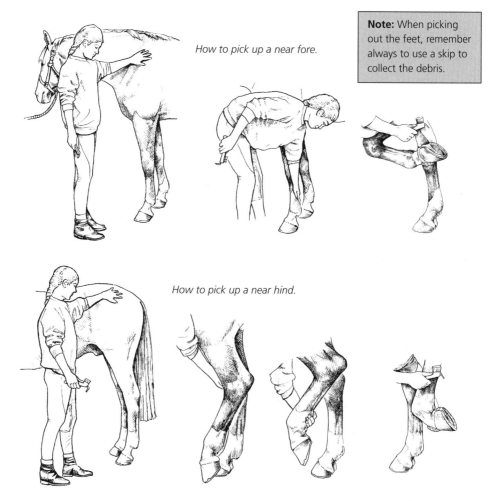

How to pick up a near fore.

Note: When picking out the feet, remember always to use a skip to collect the debris.

How to pick up a near hind.

Horses become familiar with having all four feet picked up from the near side. Safe handling of the off hind from the near side.

Care of the horse's feet should be an integral part of the daily care and management of the horse but particularly those which are stabled for much of their time.

Through regular and daily practice you must be able to:

- Pick out the horse's feet using a skip under each foot in turn to catch the dirt. (Element 6.1.1)

- Demonstrate safe procedure for picking up the feet – particularly the hind feet, which should be held in such a way that you are not at risk from the horse unexpectedly kicking back.

- Picking up all four feet from the same side, if the horse is familiar with this practice, is labour and time-saving. However, a young or unbalanced horse may require that you move around from one side to the other to pick out the feet efficiently.

- Demonstrate an awareness and competence of when to pick up all four feet from the near side and when to move around the horse.

- Manage the skip and the hoof pick with regard to overall safety and the procedure for carrying out the task competently.

- Discuss when you would wash the horse's feet, and this would include such times as returning from a muddy hack or competition or when bringing the horse in from the field. (Element 6.1.2)

- You should understand that drying the horse's heels well after washing the feet is important to prevent possible chafing or 'cracking'.

- Take care when washing feet that the horse is familiar with the process and not frightened by a running hose or bucket of water sloshing in his vicinity.

- Show an ability to oil the hooves with efficiency and safety. (Element 6.1.3) The feet should be oiled thoroughly all over the outer wall, up into the coronary band and on the soles of the feet, covering the heels and the frog. Understand the value of the use of hoof oil in maintaining the suppleness of the horn as well as giving a polished appearance to the horse.

- When commenting on the condition of a foot in front of you, look systematically for the following features (Elements 6.2.1, 6.3.1–6.3.4):

1. The snugness of the shoe to the foot; the shoe looking secure on the foot; and there being no visible signs of the clenches (nails on the outside wall of the foot) rising up and away from the wall.

2. All the clenches should be smooth, flush to the wall of the hoof and in a neat line about a third of the way up the wall from the floor.

3. The foot should not appear to be overgrowing the shoe in any area.

A foot in need of reshoeing – long toe, risen clenches, the shoe appears loose, and the heel is no longer supported by the shoe.

A good, well-shod foot – the shoe fits snugly, the clenches (nails) are flush with the hoof wall, and the heel of the shoe is long, offering good support to the horn at the heel.

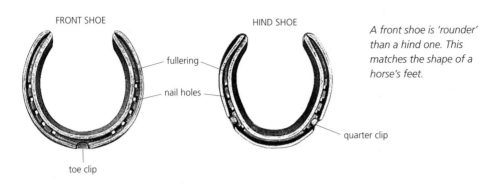

A front shoe is 'rounder' than a hind one. This matches the shape of a horse's feet.

4. The shoe should look sturdy and have no worn parts.

5. The groove in the shoe should be visible, with the nail heads well bedded down into the groove.

6. Toe or quarter clips, if present, should be flush with the wall and not dented into the foot itself.

7. The heels of the shoe should be well out in the heel region of the foot and not appear to finish short of the end of the frog.

■ Long feet (Element 6.3.2) will look as if the toe of the foot extends forward; viewed from the side, the weight of the horse will appear to be concentrated in the heel region of the foot. The hoof/pastern axis will appear to be broken backwards.

Anatomy and Handling

Know:

The main external areas (forehand, middle, hindquarters).

Basic points of the horse, their colours and markings.

How to stand a horse up correctly in the stable and/or outside.

How to lead and turn horses at walk and trot.

How to hold a reasonably quiet horse for treatment, shoeing and clipping.

ELEMENT

C	**7.1.1** Identify points of the horse.
C	**7.2.1** Use correct terminology when describing the horse's coat colour.
C	**7.2.2** Use correct terminology when describing the horse's markings.
C	**7.3.1** Show how to hold a horse for treatment.
S	**7.3.2** Show how to stand a horse up for inspection.
C	**7.4.1** Demonstrate safe, effective leading in hand at walk for an observer.
S	**7.4.2** Demonstrate safe, effective leading in hand at trot for an observer.
C	**7.4.3** Demonstrate safe, correct turning of the horse when leading in hand for an observer.

Colours

Bay A brown horse with black points. Points are the mane, tail and bottom of the horse's legs from the knees and hocks down to the hooves. Bay can be any colour brown from very light to very dark.

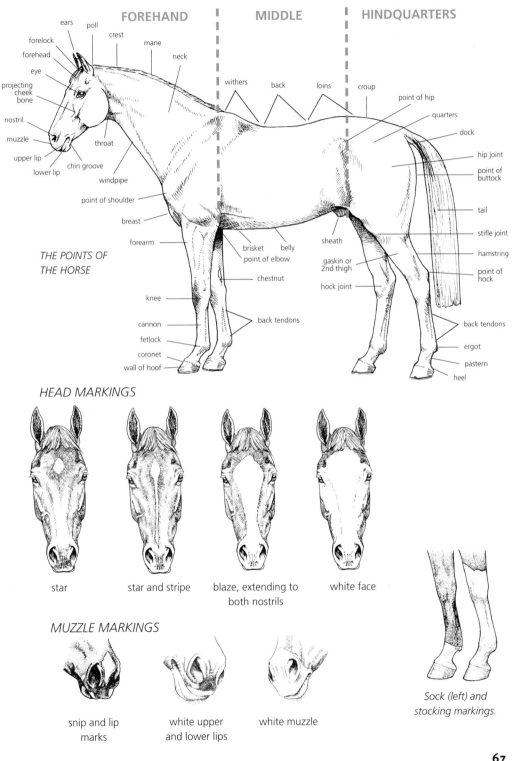

FOREHAND   MIDDLE   HINDQUARTERS

ears · poll · crest · mane · neck
forelock · forehead · eye
projecting cheek bone
nostril · muzzle · upper lip · lower lip · chin groove · throat · windpipe
point of shoulder · breast · forearm

withers · back · loins · croup · point of hip · quarters · dock · hip joint · point of buttock · tail · stifle joint · hamstring · point of hock

THE POINTS OF THE HORSE

brisket · belly · point of elbow · chestnut · knee · cannon · fetlock · coronet · wall of hoof · back tendons

sheath · gaskin or 2nd thigh · hock joint · back tendons · ergot · pastern · heel

HEAD MARKINGS

star   star and stripe   blaze, extending to both nostrils   white face

MUZZLE MARKINGS

snip and lip marks   white upper and lower lips   white muzzle

Sock (left) and stocking markings.

67

Brown Brown over most of the body with no black points.

Black A genuine black horse is very rare. Often they are dark brown or dark bay. If you cannot find any brown hairs anywhere on the horse's body then it is black.

Chestnut As with bay there are various shades of chestnut. A dark chestnut is a rich red colour all over. The most common colour chestnut is a lighter red colour all over. A liver chestnut has more of a dark brown/red colour.

Grey A grey horse is one with both black and white hairs in its coat and there are several different types of grey. Grey horses become whiter with age but their skin is always dark coloured.

- Iron grey – predominately black hairs and can appear almost black.

- Light grey – predominately white hairs.

- Dapple grey – circles of black hair over the body forming 'dapples'.

- Flea bitten grey – 'speckles' of either brown or black hair over the body.

White A white horse is like a black horse and is not a common colour. He has skin pigment that is white or pale pink and the coat is white.

Dun A dun horse has a coat that is a yellowy colour (dark or light) with black points. He may also have a black dorsal stripe along his back.

Palomino A palomino has a yellowy coloured body (from very light to golden yellow) with a light colour mane and tail.

Roan A roan has a mixture of white and other coloured hairs throughout the body.

- Strawberry roan – a mixture of red and white hairs throughout the body.

- Blue roan – black and white hairs giving a blue tinge.

- Bay roan – white and brown with black points.

- Chestnut roan/sorrel – white and chestnut with matching points. The mane and tail are similar or chestnut in colour.

Piebald Large patches of black and white over the horse. The mane and tail may be black and white.

Skewbald Large patches of any other colour than black, and white. The majority are brown and white.

Spotted/Appaloosa

- Leopard spot – large spots of any colour on a white colour.

- Blanket spot – spots on the hind quarters only.

- Snowflake – small white spots/flecks on a dark coat.

What the assessor will look for

- You should try to learn as many different colours of horses as possible and be familiar with how to identify the basic markings found on horses and how these are correctly described. This will require some book work, and then you must try and look at as many different horses as you can 'in the flesh'. If you go to a competition you could practise by looking at a horse's colours and markings and imagine describing that horse to someone who hasn't seen him. You must also learn the basic points of the horse and be able to identify these on a live horse. (Elements 7.1.1, 7.2.1 and 7.2.2)

- You will be asked to show how to hold a horse for treatment. (Element 7.3.1) It would usually be sensible to keep the horse in the stable where the confinement of the four walls may help your control. The priority for holding a horse for treatment is that you should be on the same side of the horse as the person treating the horse. If the horse throws himself about you are both able to move out of the way on the same side. If necessary, put the horse's bottom into a corner and keep him close to one of the stable walls where you can gain more control of him.

- You may be asked to hold up a front leg to help restrain the horse. In this case, stand near to the foreleg and pick up the leg, bending the knee; support the limb near the fetlock, and stand facing the horse's tail, holding the leg on the same side as the area being treated. Always give the other person a few seconds' warning if you feel you will have to let go of the leg. Try to keep your eyes on the person treating the horse, so that you are aware of what they are doing.

- If asked to stand a horse up for inspection (Element 7.3.2), it would be more

How to stand a horse up for inspection.

appropriate to bring the horse out onto the yard (as if for a vet or potential purchaser to observe). If in doubt, put a bridle on the horse. Only bring the horse out in a headcollar if you are advised that it is safe to do so. If the decision is left to you, with a horse you do not know, always choose the safe option and use a bridle. Stand the horse in the yard on as level a surface as possible. Try to make the horse stand square, taking weight on all four feet. Either stand in front of the horse with one hand on either side of the bridle, one rein in each hand facing the horse (you are then not in the observer's view), or stand close to the horse's head on the left hand side if he is fractious and likely to jump forward.

The correct way to lead a horse/pony.

How not to lead a horse/pony. Handler too far in advance – control could not be maintained.

- Leading the horse in hand (Elements 7.4.1–7.4.3) whether in walk or trot requires you to be firmly in control and to produce a lively forward-going walk or trot on a good straight line.

- When leading, always turn the horse away from you. This enables you to keep control of the hindquarters and prevent them swinging around; it also reduces the likelihood of the horse treading on you. Learn to use your voice to communicate with the horse: calm him if he is a bit full of himself and encourage him if he is lazy. With a really lazy horse it is useful to learn how to use a short whip to encourage him into more active participation.

When turning, turn the horse away from you.

- If trotting the horse in hand, you should start smoothly in walk, progress into trot, return smoothly to walk before turning, and then ease back into trot, being aware that the horse may be more forward-thinking on the return. Always make the turn in walk.

Health and Safety

Know:

The importance of physical fitness in order to carry out yard work efficiently without stress and strain.

Use correct methods for stable tasks, lifting, moving heavy weights.

How to fill, weigh and tie up a haynet.

ELEMENT

C   **8.1.1** Recognise hazardous lifting situations.

C   **8.1.2** Show safe lifting procedures.

C   **8.1.3** Show safe carrying procedures.

S   **8.2.1** Show how to fill a haynet.

S   **8.2.2** Show how to weigh a haynet.

C   **8.2.3** Show how to safely and efficiently tie up a haynet.

S   **8.2.4** Recognise potential dangers when using a haynet.

What the assessor will look for

- You should be aware that when working with horses there will be instances where your own safety and welfare is compromised if you do not carry out safe procedures when moving and lifting heavy materials.

- Lifting bales, feed sacks and full water buckets are all instances where correct lifting methods are important. (Element 8.1.1)

- When picking up a heavy weight (such as a feed sack), always bend your knees and keep your back in the vertical plane. Either take the weight of the object across your chest or put the weight onto your shoulder(s).

- When picking up full buckets of water, keep the knees bent and ideally balance one bucket by having an equal weight (another bucket) in the other hand.

- Carry bales of hay and straw in a twosome with a second person.

- If asked to fill a haynet, it is usual to shake the hay slightly (not extensively so that seed is lost) so that it is easier to stuff into the open neck of the net. (Element

How to pick up two buckets correctly.

How to pick up a feed sack – knees bent, back straight, with the weight supported on the torso.

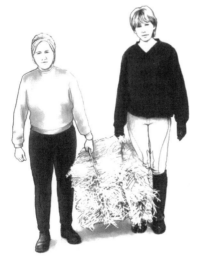

Sharing the weight of a bale, with one person on either side.

Knees bent and back straight, to individually move a bale.

8.2.1) Fill the haynet as required: small haynets may weigh 1.8kg/4lb whereas a net to last a horse overnight may hold 4.5–6.5kg/10–14lb. Close the neck by pulling the drawstring tight and weigh the net on a suspended spring-balance weighing scale. Make sure the knot in the drawstring is close to the net itself so it is out of the way when tying up. (Element 8.2.2)

- In tying up the haynet, pull the string right through the ring until the full net is tight up against the ring. Then thread the extra string through the bottom of the haynet and pull the net up as high as you can again on the ring before securing the string with a quick-release knot. This ensures that even when the net is empty it does not hang low down the wall where the horse could get a foot caught in it and be injured. Turn the net so the knot is towards the wall and less likely to be 'grabbed' by the horse. (Elements 8.2.3–8.2.4)

There is some discussion as to whether or not the haynet string should be tied directly to the ring, or whether it should be threaded through a piece of string so that it will break if the horse does get a foot caught in the net. There are points for and against each method. If the net is attached to a piece of string, the string will wear quickly and may break in the night. You should follow the regime adopted at your place of employment and be prepared to discuss both methods in your exam. The most important point is that the haynet is pulled as high as is possible when being tied up.

Horse Health

The signs of good health in horses and ponies, recognise when they are off-colour and the importance of an immediate report.

ELEMENT

S	**9.1.1**	State what you must look for at morning inspections.
S	**9.1.2**	State what you must look for at last thing at night inspections.
C	**9.2.1**	Recognise signs of good health.
C	**9.2.2**	Recognise signs of ill health.
C	**9.3.1**	Give the reasons for reporting when a horse is unwell.

The first thing you should do every morning whether your horse lives in a field or in a stable is to check that he is in good health. If you know your horse's normal behaviour then this is easier to gauge.

Signs of good health

1. Normal behaviour for that horse.

2. Alert to your presence.

3. Interested in you and his surroundings.

4. Ears pricked.

5. Breathing regularly.

6. Coat shiny and no sign of sweating.

7. There should be no discharge from his eyes or nose, and his eyes should be bright.

8.   Happy to stand on all four legs. A horse will often rest a hind leg when he is relaxed. As long as he does not always rest the same hind leg, i.e. he changes the resting leg, then there is usually nothing to worry about.

9.   His food has been eaten and his water drunk.

10. If he is in a stable his bed is not overly disturbed.

11. There is the usual amount of droppings to be found and they are of the correct consistency. Normal droppings are firm, round, separate lumps which should break apart as they hit the ground.

12. There should be no swelling of his legs.

The signs of ill health or a potential problem are the opposite of the above.

You should not be asked what a horse's normal temperature, pulse and respiration are, but it is useful to know:

Temperature: 38 °Celsius (100.5 °Fahrenheight)

Pulse (at rest): 36–42 beats per minute

Respiration (at rest): 8–12 beats per minute

- If a horse in your care appears to show any abnormal signs, as an assistant in the yard it is your job to report this immediately to a senior member of staff so they can review the situation and call a vet if necessary. The sooner a problem is spotted and dealt with the less likely a horse is to become seriously ill.

- It is important to check your horse last thing at night. If you finish the yard at about seven o'clock at night then, if he is not checked again until seven o'clock the next morning, that is a twelve-hour gap when anything could happen. If possible, horses should be checked as late as possible so that there is less time for a problem to occur.

A late night inspection should include a check that the horse is in good health and that his bed is not disturbed. If possible, it is a good idea to skip him out so that there will be less mess in the morning. His water should be checked and if he has to have a last feed or a top-up of hay or haylage this should also be done. Make sure his rugs are straight and comfortable. Lastly, check that the door is correctly secured and that the lights are off. If there is an alarm system this should be switched on.

What the assessor will look for

- The ability to recognise good health in horse(s) is an essential and basic requirement for anyone involved in the care of and responsibility for horses. Your training should have covered the various points of good and ill health and you may have been involved in or seen senior yard staff taking horses' temperatures, pulse and respiration rates, as these can be clear guides to a horse's state of well-being.

- If you are asked about early-morning inspections, the examiner would be looking for you to mention that the horse was demonstrating 'normal' behaviour. For example, you might report that the horse had eaten and drunk through the night; the stable looked 'normal', with droppings and bed disturbance no different to usual. The horse appeared at ease with himself, and greeted you over the door as you arrived, anxious for his breakfast. Everything in the stable, with the horse and in the vicinity of the yard, indicated that nothing untoward had happened during the night. (Element 9.1.1)

- Before leaving the yard at night (Element 9.1.2) last checks would include making sure that the horse was comfortable with hay as required and a full water bucket. The horse's rugs might need to be adjusted or increased according to weather conditions. Final feeds may need to be given as necessary. If horses have worked then they must be left cooled off, brushed off and rugged up appropriately. All lights and electrical appliances must be turned off, the tack room securely locked and any security alarms etc. set. Before you leave, have a final glance round to check that everything is left safe and sound.

- You will be asked about signs of good health and ill health and these may relate to a horse in front of you. (Elements 9.2.1–9.2.2).

Horse Behaviour

Show knowledge of:

The horse's natural lifestyle, instincts, actions and reactions.

ELEMENT

S	**10.1.1**	Outline the horse's lifestyle in the wild.
S	**10.2.1**	Describe the horse's basic instincts of survival.
C	**10.3.1**	Describe how to handle the horse in the stable.
C	**10.3.2**	Describe how to handle the horse in the field.
C	**10.3.3**	Describe how to handle the horse when ridden.
S	**10.4.1**	Describe signs of danger as shown in the horse's expression when in the field.
S	**10.4.2**	Describe signs of danger as shown in the horse's expression when in the stable.
S	**10.4.3**	Describe signs of danger as shown in the horse's expression when ridden.

The horse's lifestyle in the wild

The horse is a herd animal. In the wild there is safety in numbers. There is usually a dominant stallion and/or mare within the herd who will lead them and warn of approaching danger. Horses like the company of other horses although they will sort out a 'pecking order', which will usually involve fighting.

In their natural environment a herd of horses will roam in search of food and water. They are 'trickle feeders' who graze between 16 and 20 hours per day. If there is free access to water they will drink approximately twice a day.

Horses are naturally creatures of flight. If there are frightened, their immediate reaction is to run away. Only if they are cornered will they turn and fight; then they use their front and back legs, their teeth and their weight.

A horse has three basic natural instincts. In order of priority they are:

- to survive;

- to nourish (i.e. eat and drink);

- to procreate.

If they do not survive then there is no need to eat and drink, and if they are not sufficiently nourished then they will not procreate.

To ensure survival, the horse has developed many different traits. He is easily frightened. If he is frightened by something he will usually run away, but when he feels he is far enough away from the object of his fear, he will turn and look towards it. He may snort, his ears will be pricked, his tail held high and his eyes 'on stalks'. If he feels that the source of his fear is perhaps not a danger, he may well approach it and sniff it but be alert and ready to run again. If he is unable to run he is prepared to fight.

If we put this behaviour into the context of domesticated horses, then when they are in a field they are able to display this behaviour if frightened; if being ridden, they may try to bolt with the rider; and if in the stable and therefore unable to run, they may try to defend themselves by kicking and/or biting. This is one reason why it is important to approach a horse quietly, whilst talking to him. If you approach his shoulder, the horse can watch you all the way as you draw closer. If you approach his head he will lose sight of you when you are immediately in front of him because his eyes are set to the side of his head to improve rear vision.

Horses living in fields

If there is a group of horses living in a field together they will usually be calm and grazing together. If they are lying down it will usually mean that they feel safe and at ease, but there will invariably be one horse who is standing and keeping watch to ensure they are all safe. If the horses are all galloping around they may well have been scared by something or, if it is summer, be bothered by flies; one of their friends may have escaped, or they may just be having fun. Horses should always be checked if there is any kind of abnormal behaviour. A horse standing by itself, away from the others, may be feeling ill or have been injured in a fight.

It is usual to keep mares and geldings in different paddocks to help eliminate fighting. It may also be useful to separate horses and ponies so that there is less danger of injury during play or fighting. Youngstock can annoy older horses if they are living in the same field.

If a horse is used to living in a field with companions and he is left alone, he is very likely to become stressed. He could gallop around and call for his friends, and possibly even try to jump out of the field.

If two horses who are unfamiliar with each other are turned out together then they will go through a process of getting to know each other and sort out who is the boss. They will sniff and snort at each other and maybe squeal. They may strike with their front legs and/or gallop around for a short time. This behaviour will soon sort out the pecking order and they will then settle down to graze.

When turning out horses (see also page 86) is it very important that you go through a process that is safe for you and the horse. Take the horse into the field, shut the gate and turn his head towards the gate. Take off the headcollar gently but efficiently and allow him to move away from you. Do not turn your back on him as he may wheel round, buck and gallop away, especially if he has not been turned out for a while. If there is more than one horse to be turned out then the process should be the same but with everybody taking off the headcollars at the same time. To have one person left holding a horse when the others are moving away is potentially very dangerous.

When catching one horse in a field with several others do not take a bucket of food in with you. The whole group may mob you. Perhaps take a titbit in your pocket to give to the horse once you have caught him. Always approach the shoulder of the horse, talking quietly to him. Sometimes it is a good idea to put the headcollar (with the headpiece strap undone) and rope behind your back so the horse cannot see it. As you get to the horse's shoulder, talk to him again and gently put the rope round his neck. This can act as a method of control if he tries to move off. Then put the headcollar on and do it up. Stay alert for other horses being inquisitive and coming up to you and the horse you are catching. If possible, it is a good idea to take a second person with you. He or she can assist if necessary and open and close the gate for you.

A horse that is difficult to catch may be worried about being caught, having previously had a bad experience. He may only come in to work, know this and not be happy about it. He may just be being cheeky. If he is a problem to catch then, with the help of other people, you could first catch all the other horses in the field, and he may well follow them. You could make sure that whenever he is caught he is praised and given a titbit. Sometimes he should be brought in just for a feed and then turned out again so he does not always associate being caught with work. He could be turned out in a leather headcollar so that you do not have to worry about putting one on. This should be a last resort; and the headcollar must fit well and be in good condition. Learning to follow a horse's movements and body language can help in catching him and building up a relationship.

Horses living in stables

When approaching a horse in a stable you should always talk to him and, as in a field, approach the shoulder. Always tie a horse up before working around him so that you are both safe. Be aware of his body language – watch his ears, face and tail. If his ears are set back then he is angry and likely to bite or kick. If his ears are floppy, he is relaxed and comfortable with his situation. If his ears are forward then this will mean he is attentive and generally happy. If they are pricked right forward then usually something has attracted his attention and he is alert. He could move quickly, not necessarily because of you, but he may well barge you in the process or trap you against the wall or in a corner.

Whenever you are working with a horse in a stable always be alert. Because you are both in an enclosed place there is potential for you to inadvertently be trapped, trodden on or otherwise injured. Watch the horse's body language and do not make any sharp or unexpected movements. The majority of horses are kind and would not deliberately injure you – but accidents can happen. If a horse leans towards you there is a chance he will then move his foot towards you. If your foot is in the way he cannot see it and will accidentally tread on it.

Horses thrive on routine and consistent handling. A horse that is new on a yard will often feel insecure and will show his apprehension by becoming fractious. He may whinny, dash around in the box and generally be unsettled. Making sure he has food in the box may help, and putting him where he can see another quiet horse may also be useful. He should settle within a day or two and a regular routine and calm, sympathetic handling will play a major role in this.

A horse that is used to being in a stable will spend his time eating, lying down and generally appearing relaxed. He may spend many hours just looking over his stable door watching the world go by.

A well-behaved horse in a stable will move away from the door as you enter and be happy to have his headcollar on and be tied up. He will pick up his feet and move over when asked. He will not try to bite and kick you but will enjoy the attention he is receiving.

A badly behaved horse in a stable may put his head in the corner, so his bottom is towards you, and then try to kick. His body language including his eyes, ears and tail will tell you whether he is a danger or not. If you ever feel unsafe in a horse's box it is always better to go out and tell your supervisor about the problem.

The horse when being ridden

When a horse is being ridden his natural instinct of flight from a predator can create problems. He may well try to bolt from something he does not like. He will, at the very least, shy away from spooky things. You can use his herd instinct to good effect though, and being ridden out in the company of braver horses can help a green or frightened horse. He will follow them and start to learn that life is not as frightening as he thought it was. Whenever you are out hacking, though, you should be alert as a stray plastic bag may be just round the corner, or a pheasant can fly out of a hedge at you.

A horse with a good temperament will be honest and genuine. He will do everything asked of him to the best of his ability and will not be nappy and bad tempered. The majority of horses are kind and enjoy the company of humans. These kinds of horse are good for novice riders to learn to ride on as their behaviour is more predictable. Those who tend to try to bite or kick you or who are fractious or unsettled have often had bad experiences with humans and need to rebuild their trust in people.

A fresh horse is invariably a fit horse, one that has not had enough exercise for the amount of food he is receiving. He will be very keen when he comes out of the box and may not stand still to be mounted. He may jog, shy at things, and when he goes into canter may try to go faster than you want him to and buck. If he is turned out in the field during the day as well as being ridden then this may be avoided.

Horses are generally kind, amenable animals and this is one of the main reasons they have become domesticated. Because they are creatures of flight they should, however, never be taken for granted because even the most reliable of horses can be upset by something different. You must always be alert and consistent when working around horses to get the best from them and build up a good relationship.

What the assessor will look for

This section is assessed in the theory exam, where you will be in a group of up to six others.

- Be confident, giving clear concise answers to any questions on the topic.

- If you are unsure about the answer to a question, do not make up a 'spur of the moment' answer. Be truthful and say you do not know.

- Be involved in the general discussion. It is easy to let your concentration wander.

- Listen to other candidates' answers and be prepared to offer further information if asked.

- Do not appear over-confident or superior to your fellow candidates.

Basic Grassland Care

Know:

What to look for in and around the field.

Daily inspections.

How to turn out a horse, how to catch him and bring him in from the field.

Recognise a horse-sick field.

ELEMENT

| S | **11.1.1** Describe a 'horse-sick' field. |

11.1.1 Describe a 'horse-sick' field.

11.1.2 Give ways a horse-sick field can be avoided/remedied.

11.2.1 Describe what to check each day in the field.

11.3.1 Describe acceptable, safe methods of turning a horse out into a field.

11.3.2 Describe acceptable, safe methods of bringing a horse in from the field.

What the assessor will look for

- You must be able to discuss and describe a 'horse-sick' field. (Element 11.1.1) The assessor would expect you to know that the following would be indicative of 'horse-sick' pasture:

  1. Too many horses or ponies on a relatively small patch of land.

  2. Many piles of droppings scattered around the pasture.

  3. Patches of smooth, well-grazed 'bowling green' areas of grass with few droppings interspersed by patches of rank, dark-green, long grass where the horses have fouled and will not eat the developing 'leggy' grass.

4. An abundance of nettles and docks and other hardy weeds (often ragwort) which deplete the grass and may be harmful to the horses.

5. Often 'horse-sick' pasture may also have neglected or unsuitable fencing around it.

- Horse-sick pasture can be avoided by not over-grazing and good management. Rotation of paddocks gives the pasture a chance to rest and regrow and ensures that is not constantly overgrazed. Sensible stocking levels avoid putting too many horses on too small an area of grassland. Regular removal of droppings (preferably by picking them up by hand, removal with a vacuum-type machine or harrowing to spread them) alleviates the tendency for uneven and poor grazing patches to establish (some areas become overgrazed while others are covered in droppings and then a rank covering of untouched, tainted grass). Cross-grazing with other animals will also sweeten the pasture and reduce the risk of it becoming sick. (Element 11.1.2)

- Daily checks of pasture should include checking the fencing for safety and repair, noting the state of the grass, and making sure that the gate is secure and that shelter and water supply are in a good state. Keep a watchful eye for the

Ragwort – this poisonous plant has yellow daisy-like, multi-headed flowers and serrated leaves.

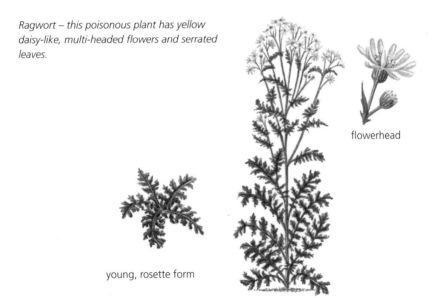

flowerhead

young, rosette form

appearance of any poisonous plants or dangerous objects which could harm the horses. (Element 11.2.1)

■ When turning horses out, the safety of handler and horse is of paramount concern. Horses may be enthusiastic about returning to the field and therefore you must minimise the risk of being injured by their joy at returning to freedom. Always take enough people to manage the number of horses you are turning out, the number required depending on the horses' manner and behaviour. One person may easily turn out three or four quiet ponies, whereas it would be wise to have one person per horse with two or three fit, competition horses being turned out for some exercise. In general terms:

1. Open the gate and make sure that all people and horses/ponies are in the field and the gate has been closed again.

2. Make sure that the handlers are in their own space and that they have turned their horses' heads back to face the closed gate.

3. Make sure that everyone releases their horse(s) at the same time, so that all the horses run off together – but first they have to make a turn. This avoids the tendency for them to kick up their heels (in your face) and run away violently.

4. Make sure that the gate is securely closed as you leave. (Element 11.3.1)

■ When bringing horses in from the field (Element 11.3.2), the same criteria would apply for numbers. The number of horses/ponies that can be safely managed depends extensively on the type and fitness of the animals and on the competence and experience of the handlers.

■ An experienced person would be more able to manage several horses than an inexperienced, less confident person.

■ If taking food to entice the horse(s) be very careful that it does not incite a horse's natural instinctive reaction to display dominance or 'pecking order' traits. Do not take a bucket with food in; instead have a titbit or two in your pocket.

■ Food, if used, must be offered discreetly, as the horse is approached from the front but slightly towards the shoulder or neck. Introduce the rope of the headcollar around the horse's neck and then apply the headcollar, attaching the strap securely.

- Lead the horse(s) to the gate and bring them out, being careful to keep any remaining animals in the field and closing the gate securely. Bring horses in in an orderly way, not getting too close to each other and making sure that you have prepared somewhere for the horses to go when they come into the yard. (Element 11.3.2)

Watering and Feeding

Know:

General principles and the importance of cleanliness.

The various types of fodder in general use and recognise good and bad quality feed.

Suitable feeding of horses and ponies in light work.

(Definition of 'light work': daily walk, trot and canter where the horse is not stressed.)

ELEMENT

C	**12.1.1**	Name oats, barley, sugar-beet, bran, coarse mix, nuts/cubes, chaff.
S	**12.1.2**	Recognise good quality oats, barley, sugar-beet pulp/cubes, bran, coarse mix, nuts/cubes, chaff.
S	**12.1.3**	Recognise poor quality oats, barley, sugar-beet pulp/cubes, bran, coarse mix, nuts/cubes, chaff.
S	**12.2.1**	Recognise good quality hay.
S	**12.2.2**	Recognise bad quality hay.
S	**12.2.3**	Recognise acceptable quality hay.
S	**12.3.1**	Recognise good quality haylage.
S	**12.3.2**	Recognise bad quality haylage.
C	**12.4.1**	Discuss the dangers of feeding poor quality fodder.
C	**12.5.1**	Give the rules of good feeding.
C	**12.6.1**	Give the rules of watering.
S	**12.6.2**	Know the importance of cleanliness.

C **12.7.1** Discuss suitable feed for a grass-kept horse and/or pony in light work throughout the seasons.

C **12.7.2** Discuss suitable daily quantity of feed for a grass-kept horse and/or pony in light work throughout the seasons.

C **12.8.1** Discuss suitable feed for a stabled horse and/or pony in light work.

C **12.8.2** Discuss suitable daily quantity of feed for a stabled horse and/or pony in light work.

C **12.9.1** Discuss suitable methods of watering horses at grass.

S **12.9.2** Discuss suitable methods of feeding horses at grass.

You need to be able to recognise feedstuffs in general use. You also need to be able to assess whether feed samples are good quality or poor. To assess a sample look at it and if it is in a jar take the lid off. It is not a good idea to put your nose in the jar,

Various common foodstuffs.

whole oats

whole barley

coarse mix

bran

nuts/cubes

chaff/chop

sugar-beet shreds

sugar-beet cubes

but a bad sample will smell musty. You do not particularly want to inhale this. A bad sample will also usually be of a dull colour, and may be dusty or even mouldy. It may also be damp. A food that shows any of these characteristics should not be fed to a horse. He may not eat it, but if he does it could give him colic; if it is dusty it could lead to respiratory problems.

You also need to be able to recognise good and poor quality hay and haylage.

- Good hay is a bright colour, has a sweet smell, and long stalks with some flowers or seed heads on them. There would be no weeds or foreign bodies in good quality hay.

- Poor quality hay displays the opposite characteristics. It may be mouldy, dusty and a dark colour with a musty, foul smell.

- Acceptable hay may not be as sweet smelling or as bright as good hay; but it must be dust and mould free.

- Good quality haylage is similar to good quality hay. It usually has a stronger smell than hay as there is more water content in the grass when it is cut than there is in hay. There should still be no mould. If the plastic wrapping in which haylage is packed is pierced then the whole bale may be of no use. Once opened a bale of haylage should be used within three to five days.

Rules of feeding

It is important to learn the rules of feeding and to understand why they are important.

1. Feed according to size, age, body weight, type, temperament, time of year, type of work to be done and the level of rider that will be riding him.

If a horse is overfed it can lead to any of the following: obesity, joint and leg problems, digestive disorders, laminitis, behaviour problems.

If a horse is underfed then it will not be able to perform well and will lose weight.

2. Feed little and often.

A horse has a small stomach relative to its overall size. The stomach is about the size of a rugby ball. A horse is designed to be a trickle feeder (i.e. eats little and often). By feeding little and often you are mimicking his natural lifestyle.

3. Always feed good quality food.

Feeding poor quality food can lead to digestive and respiratory disorders. It also has less feeding value. Some horses will not eat poor quality food and will therefore lose condition and not be able to do their job of work.

4. Feed plenty of bulk.

A horse's natural feed is grass. Consequently its digestive system is used to bulk. Without this the digestive system cannot work efficiently and digestive problems can result.

5. Do not make any sudden changes to the type of food being fed.

The bacteria that break down the food in a horse's digestive system are 'food specific'. If you feed a lot of barley and a small amount of sugar beet the horse will have a lot of 'barley bacteria' and a small amount of 'sugar beet bacteria'. If you suddenly change to a large amount of oats there will be insufficient bacteria to break this down adequately. The most likely result will be colic. If you make gradual changes to the feed then the bacteria have an opportunity to multiply.

6. Always use clean utensils and bowls.

Horses are notoriously 'fussy feeders' and unclean utensils can put them off. You would not want to eat from a dirty plate. Also there is a possibility of spreading disease.

7. Feed a hard feed at least an hour before exercise, and longer for demanding work.

A horse's stomach is located close to its diaphragm. When full, the stomach can restrict the movement of the diaphragm. Also, trying both to digest food and to produce energy for muscular action could overload the body's systems.

8. Feed at regular times daily.

Horses are creatures of habit and thrive best when they have a routine.

9. Feed something succulent every day.

Apples, carrots and other succulents help keep a stabled horse happy. They add variety to the diet as well as providing extra vitamins.

10. Water before feeding.

This is a rather outdated rule and comes from a time when horses used to be taken to a trough to drink and did not have constant free access to water. A horse would gulp down water after feeding and this would wash the food through his system before it was all digested. Nowadays we know that horses should have free access to fresh water. Then they usually do not feel the necessity to gulp down large amounts of water after they have eaten their hard feed.

Rules of watering

You will also be questioned on the rules of watering.

1. A horse should have a constant access to a clean supply of fresh water at all times.

An adult horse's body is about 65% water and a lack of water can lead to dehydration.

2. Do not give a very hot horse a large drink straight after work.

His system will not be able to take it and it can lead to metabolic problems.

3. Ensure all water containers are kept very clean.

A horse must not be discouraged from drinking and a dirty container can turn the water 'sour'.

4. If the horse is using buckets then change the water at least twice a day.

There is a chemical reaction in water that is left standing and this produces ammonia, which will discourage a horse from drinking.

5. Drinking containers should be large enough for a horse to get his muzzle in comfortably.

6. If travelling to a competition it is sensible to take your own water.

Firstly, you then know you have some to use, and secondly, the horse will be used to that particular type of water and will not be put off drinking.

7. Try to be aware of approximately how much water per day your horse drinks.

This can only really be measured if you use buckets or are lucky enough to have water monitors on automatic bowls.

There are various ways that water can be supplied to horses. **In a stable** the two most popular ways are buckets and automatic bowls.

- **Buckets** can be easily cleaned and you can see how much the horse is drinking. You can restrict water intake if this is necessary and add medicine to the water. They are, however, very labour intensive and can be heavy to carry around. They can also be knocked over by the horse and he will then be without water until he is checked. If you put buckets in a tyre to stabilise them this will take up a lot of room in a stable. Some people clip them to the wall at breast height, but this is not a natural drinking position for the horse.

- **Automatic bowls** are very labour saving and ensure that the horse has a constant supply of water. They can freeze in winter if the pipes are not well lagged. The pipes also need to be protected from the horse so that he does not chew them. Unless there are expensive water monitors on the pipe, it is not possible to measure how much the horse is drinking and it is difficult to restrict water if this is necessary. It can be difficult to keep them clean too. An automatic bowl needs to be carefully and securely sited within the stable so that the horse does not damage it.

Horses and ponies living at grass need access to clean fresh water just as much as stabled horses do. The best way to provide this is by a self-filling trough that is set away from the field entrance and overhanging trees. A free-flowing stream through a field may sound like an ideal way of providing water, but the stream may be polluted. It must also be remembered that if a stream has a sandy bed a horse may ingest sand and eventually get sand colic. Also, the approaches to the stream may become very poached and potentially dangerous.

A safe trough with no rough edges can be suitable but it will need filling up regularly. Old bath tubs and containers with sharp edges must not be used unless they are boxed in so the horses are protected from the edges.

Using buckets in a field is not a good idea as they are easily knocked over. It is also very labour intensive to keep them topped up. If, however, there is no other option then buckets will be necessary as a horse must have water.

The importance of cleanliness (Element 12.6.2) follows on from the provision of fresh water in clean utensils. Cleanliness refers not only to watering but to feeding as well. Cleanliness is of the utmost importance in any well-run riding establishment. Maintaining cleanliness is in the interests of all the horses' health and well-being and is likely to inhibit the proliferation of vermin.

How much to feed?

Assessing how much feed to give a horse comes with practice, but first you need to understand the basic concept that the horse, when left to his own devices in a field and not working, will eat 100% bulk (grass or hay). When we start to work him he may well need extra nutrients to give him the energy to sustain his work. As a horse works harder he will need more of the 100% of his total intake as hard/concentrate food.

When talking about feeding horses and ponies it is important to remember that each horse is an individual. Each horse/pony needs to be observed daily to check his condition and behaviour. What is right for one horse may not be so for another horse of similar height and build.

For Stage 1 you will be discussing feeding for horses/ponies in light work. This is generally taken as a horse or pony that is doing about one hour of work a day – walk, trot and a small amount of canter.

A horse being fed good grass and/or good hay may well be able to undertake this work without any hard feed at all. If he needs any hard feed it may only be 10% of his total food intake. For example, let's take a horse of about 16 hh. He will eat in total about 30lbs of food per day (13.6kg). The only correct way to determine how much food in total a horse needs daily is to weigh him. A horse eats approximately $2^1/_2$% of his body weight per day. You can, however, approximate his weight by using a weigh tape or by applying one of several different formulae.

Possibly the easiest way is to remember the following approximate figures:

> 16 hh – 30lbs (13.6kg)
>
> 15 hh – 26lbs (11.7kg)
>
> 14 hh – 22lbs (9.9kg)
>
> 13 hh – 18lbs (8.1kg)
>
> 12 hh – 14lbs (6.3kg)

These are a rough guide but they give you a basis from which to work in the exam.

So if you are going to feed the 16 hh horse in light work 10% hard food and 90%

bulk he would receive 3lbs (1.36kg) of hard food and 27lbs (12.24kg) of bulk (hay and/or grass). It may be better, if it is possible, to split the hard food into two small feeds during the day. If he is stabled then it would be a good idea for him to have three nets of hay a day, with the largest one at night. Hopefully he would go out in a field for a few hours a day and how much he would eat in the field would depend on how much grass there was. This would have to be approximated. Some horses may require a little more hard food for light work – up to 15%, but rarely more than this.

It is probably best to feed a horse in light work either horse and pony nuts or a coarse mix. Both these types of food are classed as 'complete', which means they are carefully formulated to ensure the correct nutrients are present. This can make feeding less complicated and means you do not have lots of different bags open. Some people add some kind of chaff to hard feed to help the horse chew more slowly and not gorge his feed.

A native pony in light work will probably not need any concentrate feed for most of the year. If he is at grass this may well need to be restricted in the spring and autumn so that he does not contract laminitis. He will probably need hay twice a day in the winter and possibly a small hard feed of pony nuts.

A horse in light work living at grass all year round would need the grass supplemented by hay during the months when the grass is not growing and will probably require a little hard food.

Feeding horses in fields

When feeding horses at grass consideration for your own safety is vital. It is better not to feed concentrate feed in the field. If possible bring the horses into the yard to feed hard feed. If this is not possible then get some help to undertake the task. Put the feeds well enough apart so that the horses cannot kick each other. It may be worth seeing if you can (with your assistants) just put the feed bowls through the fence so that you do not have to go into the field. If there is one horse that is bullied or eats more slowly then take him out of the field and feed him separately.

When putting out hay always set down at least one more pile than the number of horses. This is so that if a horse is bullied away from a pile he will have another one to go to. Make sure the piles are far enough apart so that the horses cannot kick or bully each other.

What the assessor will look for

- Try to make sure that you are familiar with recognising different types of feed in 'your' feed room, and in any other yard where you might have the chance to look at the feeds in use there.

- The feeds listed in Element 12.1.1 should be familiar to you.

- Learn the rules for feeding so that you know them off by heart. (Element 12.5.1) They are the foundation from which you will feed horses of all types throughout your time of working with and caring for equines.

- Knowledge of suitable methods of feeding horses and ponies at grass (Element 12.9.2) is expected. Discuss how 'pecking order' affects group feeding, with the possibility of some horses being bullied.

- You will be in a group situation and must present yourself confidently, ready to discuss the aspects of watering and feeding required.

- Listen carefully to the questions and the answers given by other candidates. Be prepared to add further information if required.

- If you do not understand a question always ask the assessor to repeat it. It is important you understand – you might give an answer to a question that actually has not been asked. This can make your answer sound incorrect.

General Knowledge

Know:

The risks and responsibilities involved when riding or leading on the public highway.

The correct procedures in the event of an accident.

Safety rules and fire precautions.

The British Horse Society's aims.

C	**13.1.1**	Describe suitable clothes to wear when working with horses.
C	**13.2.1**	Describe fire precautions in the work place.
C	**13.3.1**	Give the correct procedure in the event of an accident to a person.
S	**13.4.1**	Give the safety rules for riding in a class.
C	**13.4.2**	Give the rules and good manners involved when taking horses on the public highway.
S	**13.5.1**	Give the aims of The British Horse Society.

What the assessor will look for

- You should know that safe footwear is of paramount importance when working around horses. Sturdy shoes or boots (never soft shoes or trainers) are what is needed. Flapping or loose fashion clothing is unsuitable. Gloves and riding hats are an added precaution when handling young or unruly horses. Jewellery should be minimal (a watch, wedding ring) or preferably not worn at all. Avoid strong perfume which can excite horses. You should be warm, dry and able to move easily in whatever you wear. In the working environment you should look neat, tidy and professional. (Element 13.1.1)

- Everyone working in the establishment should be briefed in fire precautions and fire drill for the centre. These should include a strict 'no smoking' policy anywhere in the yard. There should be fire extinguishers in small areas, such as the tack room and office, and fire-fighting equipment, such as hoses permanently attached to a water supply, for large areas of the yard. There should be an alarm, to which everyone reacts, and fire points for everyone to gather at. There should be a system for quickly turning horses out into nearby paddocks in the event of a fire. Everyone should have a clear understanding of how to call the fire brigade – by dialling 999 and giving details and directions. (Element 13.2.1)

- Feel very sure that you could carry out an acceptable procedure in the event of someone in your yard suffering an accident (Element 13.3.1):

1. Remain calm.

2. Assess the situation and go first to the injured person (call for assistance if you think you may need it – but you should not be in sole charge at this level).

3. Encourage the casualty to stay still and not hurry to get up (he or she may be winded, shocked or even have broken a limb).

4. Reassure the person; if necessary, keep them warm with a coat (if necessary, use your own) or a blanket and encourage them to breathe deeply and stay still.

5. Follow the instructions of the person in charge.

6. Know how to call an ambulance if one is necessary. In the UK that means dialling 999. Give the location as clearly as you can and a brief explanation of the accident and casualty.

7. After the incident has been dealt with, make sure that when the accident book is completed, you sign the record as being a witness to the incident, checking that everything is clearly and correctly recorded. This should be done as soon after the accident as possible.

- When riding in a class lesson you should always mount safely, preferably with everyone in an orderly line so that the horses are well spaced and no horse can interfere with another. Whether riding in closed or open order (closed order is when you work as a ride, one behind the other; open order is when you work by yourself in the school but with others around) make sure that you never get too close to another horse. If you have to pass another horse from any direction, always allow enough space and try not to take another horse and rider by surprise. If in doubt, let them know you are close. Always pass other riders left hand to left hand, and give way to a faster pace, i.e. if you are in walk then give way to a rider coming behind you in trot. If one rider is having trouble with his horse, give him extra space until he has regained his control and calmness. If there is an incident where a rider falls off, the whole ride should halt until the problem is resolved. (Element 13.4.1)

- Rules and good manners involved with taking horses on the public highway (Element 13.4.2) would include:

1. Always being aware of and courteous to other road users.

2. Thanking anyone who slows down for you. Acknowledge with a smile or nod, even if you cannot take your hand off the reins.

3. Being aware of what is going on around you. Make clear signals to others as to your intentions.

4. Wearing 'hi-viz' clothing and equipment on yourself and your horse so that you are easily visible to other road users.

5. Riding carefully, in single file, unless the road is wide enough and the visibility is good enough for it to be safe to use double file.

6. Never riding on a pavement or footpath (it is illegal to do so in the UK). If there are pedestrians nearby, they may be frightened by the size of the horse.

7. Never riding on ornamental grass verges or on any areas where someone has obviously taken trouble to maintain the grass in lawn condition.

8. If leading a horse on the highway, it must wear a bridle. You should place yourself between the horse and the traffic, leading it in the same direction as the traffic is travelling (i.e. in the UK that would mean leading on the left-hand side of the road with you on the right-hand side of the horse).

HAND SIGNALS

'I'm turning left.'

'I'm turning right.'

'Slow down.'

'Stop.'

Check behind for traffic before moving out to pass a parked car.

If leading on the road, the horse must wear a bridle. Place yourself between the horse and the traffic, and lead in the same direction as the traffic. Wear a fluorescent tabard.

- You should know that The British Horse Society is the biggest charity membership organisation whose aims are the interests and welfare of the horse. (Element 13.5.1) The Society works hard in the following areas:

1. Welfare.

2. Education and training, including administering the examination system, which regulates instructor qualifications, and the Register of Instructors and the Register of Grooms.

3. Safety.

4. Rights of way and access.

5. The BHS approves riding schools and livery yards across the UK and abroad.

6. Competitions and tourism.

7. The BHS has a nationwide system of British Riding Clubs which are affiliated to the Society.

Stage 1
Riding

Syllabus

Candidates must be capable of riding a quiet, experienced horse or pony in an enclosed space. Their balance and security should indicate the correct foundation for future progress.

Candidates who are considered to be well below the standard may be asked to retire.

IMPORTANT: Candidates are advised to check that they are working from the latest examination syllabus, as examination content and procedure are liable to alteration. Contact the BHS Examinations Office for up-to-date information regarding the syllabus.

STAGE ONE - Syllabus

Stage 1 - Riding

Candidates must be physically fit in order to carry out the selected tasks and topics efficiently without undue stress and strain and they will be expected to demonstrate competent use of time. Candidates are required to demonstrate their ability to ride a quiet, experienced horse or pony in an enclosed space without assistance. Their balance and security should indicate the correct foundation for future progress. *Candidates who are considered to be well below the standard may be asked to retire.*

Unit code number S1RIDI

Learning Outcomes *The candidate should be able to:*	Element	Assessment criteria *The candidate has achieved this outcome because s/he can:*	Influence
Demonstrate: Leading a saddled and bridled horse in hand, from either side. Checking saddlery for its fitting and soundness.	1.1.1	Demonstrate safe, effective leading in hand at walk	Compulsory
	1.2.1	Demonstrate safe, effective leading in hand at trot	Supporting
	1.3.1	Demonstrate safe, correct turning of the horse when leading in hand	Compulsory
	1.4.1	Carryout appropriate tack checking procedures prior to mounting	Supporting
Demonstrate: Mounting and dismounting from the ground, and from a mounting block.	2.1.1	Demonstrate correct mounting from a mounting block	Compulsory
	2.2.1	Demonstrate correct mounting from the ground	Supporting
	2.3.1	Demonstrate correct dismounting	Compulsory
Demonstrate: Taking up and adjusting stirrups and reins. Checking and tightening girths.	3.1.1	Carry out correct girth adjusting procedures prior to riding away	Compulsory
	3.2.1	Carry out correct stirrup adjusting procedures prior to riding away	Compulsory
	3.3.1	Demonstrate correct placement of stirrup leathers	Supporting
	3.4.1	Demonstrate correct method of holding the rein	Supporting
Show the correct basics in the ability to maintain a correct, balanced position when riding with stirrups.	4.1.1	Show a correct, secure and balanced position at walk with stirrups at a suitable length for riding on the flat	Compulsory
	4.2.1	Show a correct, secure and balanced position at trot with stirrups at a suitable length for riding on the flat	Compulsory
	4.3.1	Show a correct, secure and balanced position at canter with stirrups at a suitable length for riding on the flat	Supporting
Show the correct basics in the ability to maintain a correct, balanced position when riding without stirrups.	5.1.1	Show a correct, secure and balanced position at walk without stirrups	Compulsory
	5.2.1	Show a correct, secure and balanced position at trot without stirrups	Compulsory
Show the correct basics in the ability to maintain a correct, balanced position in preparation for jumping.	6.1.1	Maintain a correct, secure and balanced position at the rising trot and in the jumping seat with stirrups at a suitable length	Compulsory
	6.2.1	Maintain a correct, secure and balanced position at the canter in the jumping seat with stirrups at a suitable length	Supporting
Show the correct basics in the ability to maintain a correct, balanced position when working over poles.	7.1.1	Demonstrate a correct, secure and balanced position at the trot in the light balanced jumping seat with stirrups at a suitable length over ground poles	Compulsory
Show a basic understanding of the natural aids.	8.1.1	Demonstrate the natural aids for riding the horse forward correctly	Compulsory
	8.2.1	Demonstrate the natural aids for riding correct circles	Supporting
	8.3.1	Demonstrate the natural aids for riding correct turns	Supporting
	8.4.1	Demonstrate the natural aids for riding correct straight lines	Supporting
Know the reasons for trotting on named diagonals.	9.1.1	Demonstrate an ability to rise with correct diagonals	Compulsory
Know an incorrect leading leg in canter and trot to enable a correct lead to be established.	10.1.1	Demonstrate an ability to recognise cantering with the correct leading leg	Compulsory
	10.1.2	Uses corners/ half circles to help ensure correct strike-offs into canter	Compulsory
Know how to handle the reins.	11.1.1	Show a correctly maintained rein contact throughout	Supporting
Know how to handle a whip.	12.1.1	Demonstrate correct use of a whip which does not exceed 75 centimetres (30 inches)	Supporting

Riding

Demonstrate

Leading a saddled and bridled horse in hand, from either side.

Checking saddlery for its fitting and soundness.

ELEMENT

C	**1.1.1**	Demonstrate safe, effective leading in hand at walk.
S	**1.2.1**	Demonstrate safe, effective leading in hand at trot.
C	**1.3.1**	Demonstrate safe, correct turning of the horse when leading in hand.
S	**1.4.1**	Carry out appropriate tack-checking procedures prior to mounting.

What the assessor will look for

- We have discussed leading the horse in hand in the care section (pages 70-71) and all the same principles apply here. (Elements 1.1.1, 1.2.1 and 1.3.1)

- It is necessary that you are competent in leading the horse from both sides as there may be a requirement for you to lead the horse on a public highway at

Leading the horse in hand. The stirrups are run up and the reins taken over the horse's head.

Leading in hand. This horse is wearing a running martingale so the leader leaves the reins over the neck and leads as shown.

some time. In this latter case you would lead the horse on the near side of the road, placing yourself between the traffic and the horse (i.e. leading the horse on the offside) (see page 100). When you are leading a horse in a bridle, take the reins over the head (unless the horse is wearing a martingale, in which case you would lead with the reins in place around the horse's neck). If leading for some distance make sure that the girth is firm and the stirrups are run up and cannot slip down.

■ Before mounting, check the girth and tighten it a little, if necessary. Make sure that the reins are over the horse's head ready to mount, and at that point just

Uncomfortable bridle – bit too low, browband pinching the base of the ears, and noseband too high and pressing against the cheekbone.

Uncomfortable bridle – bit too high, browband pinching the base of the ears, and noseband too high and pressing against the cheekbone.

The bridle looks comfortable for the horse: the bit just wrinkles the corner of the mouth, the noseband is about two fingers' width below the cheekbone, and the browband allows room around the base of the ears.

check that the bridle looks comfortable and the horse is at ease. Pull down the stirrups so that they are ready for use when mounting – you can roughly estimate your stirrup length by putting the iron up under your armpit. Check the stirrups from in front of the horse to see that they are hanging level.

Estimating stirrup length. Put your arm through the reins while carrying out this procedure, unless the horse is tied up or being held by someone else.

Demonstrate:

Mounting and dismounting from the ground and/or from a mounting block.

ELEMENT

| C | **2.1.1** Demonstrate correct mounting from a mounting block. |

| S | **2.2.1** Demonstrate correct mounting from the ground. |

| C | **2.3.1** Demonstrate correct dismounting. |

What the assessor will look for

- Mounting correctly and well is in the interests of the horse's welfare as well as your own. It is a very important part of developing skill as a rider. You should have been taught to mount well and correctly at the outset of your riding experience, and this skill should stay with you throughout your riding life. There will be many occasions (particularly for older riders) when it is appropriate to mount using a mounting block, but nevertheless the ability to mount in an agile way, not inconveniencing the horse, should be of paramount importance. If we discuss some of the reasons why mounting is so important, this will give you a clear idea of why examiners consider competence in this (perhaps small) part of the Stage 1 exam to be of high value. (Elements 2.1.1 and 2.2.1)

If you learn to mount athletically and well, the horse will benefit in the following ways:

  - You will unbalance him less because you are agile and in control of your body weight.

  - You will spring up from the ground and lower your weight gently into the saddle.

  - You will avoid ever touching him with your right leg as it passes over his rump.

  - By springing up and putting your hand well onto the offside of the saddle, you will avoid pulling the saddle towards you and risking the saddle slipping or the

Mounting from the ground.

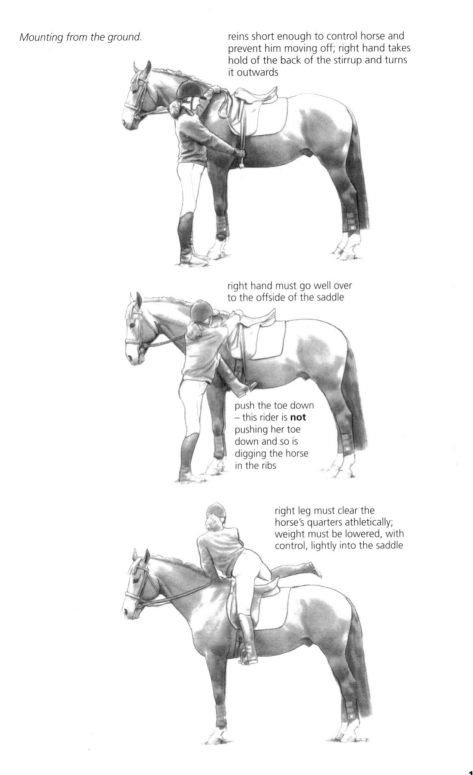

reins short enough to control horse and prevent him moving off; right hand takes hold of the back of the stirrup and turns it outwards

right hand must go well over to the offside of the saddle

push the toe down – this rider is **not** pushing her toe down and so is digging the horse in the ribs

right leg must clear the horse's quarters athletically; weight must be lowered, with control, lightly into the saddle tree being twisted by the strain put onto it.

- You are less likely to cause the horse to tense and dip away from your weight, or, worse still, to tighten his back and try to run away or buck as you sit down on him.

Poor mounting technique can ultimately injure the horse's back, damage the saddle, damage the rider's back, and create tension and an unsettled reaction in the horse, which could cause an accident.

- Whether mounting from the ground or from a mounting block the same principles apply. From a mounting block there is obviously less need to spring. The horse should stand still while you mount (if necessary, the horse should be held beside the mounting block by an assistant). You must keep the reins short enough in your left hand to control the horse and keep him still.

- The assessor will also be watching you dismount. As with all exercises you must adopt a safe procedure.

  - Make sure you have a contact on both reins and then put both reins into your left hand. If you have a whip, this should also be in your left hand, down the horse's left shoulder.

  - Put your right hand on the pommel of the saddle and take both your feet out of the stirrups.

  - Lean forward a little and throw your right leg clear, over the horse's rump, and land close to your horse on the near side facing forwards.

  - Keep hold of the reins in your left hand and run up your stirrups. When you are ready, take the left rein with your right hand (close to the bit) and stand facing forwards.

Demonstrate:

Taking up and adjusting stirrups and reins.

Checking and tightening girths.

ELEMENT

C	**3.1.1** Carry out correct girth adjusting procedures prior to riding away.
C	**3.2.1** Carry out correct stirrup adjusting procedures prior to riding away.
S	**3.3.1** Demonstrate correct placement of stirrup leathers.
S	**3.4.1** Demonstrate correct method of holding the rein.

Checking the girth whilst in the saddle.

Tightening the girth whilst in the saddle.

Adjusting the stirrup length whilst in the saddle. Throughout the rider keeps his/her feet in the irons for security.

What the assessor will look for

- Once mounted, you should be proficient in checking your girth from the saddle and be able to tighten it if necessary. Slide your leg well forward, keeping your foot in the stirrup, and keep your reins short so that you can control the horse; stay relaxed and balanced as you pull up the saddle flap to expose the girth straps. If there is a buckle guard, make sure it is pulled down smoothly over the buckles once you have tightened the girth. (Element 3.1.1) If, after riding around for a few minutes, you feel the girth needs a final check and adjustment, then ask to turn in and recheck it.

- Your stirrups should be level. Hang your leg alongside the stirrup and the base of the stirrup iron should be in the vicinity of your ankle bone. If your stirrups need adjusting then do this with your foot loosely in the iron, pull the leather up and then use the pressure of your foot on the iron to slide the leather back into place. (Element 3.2.1) If, after riding for a few minutes, your stirrups feel unlevel or too short/long then ask if you may turn in and alter them. You must feel comfortable. Learning to ride with a stirrup that feels 'right' for you takes time and 'feel'. If you are nervous or tense then you are less likely to 'let down' into your stirrups as well as on a day when you feel confident and relaxed. Whenever you are anxious (e.g. on the first horse in your exam) it may be wise to have your stirrups one hole shorter than 'normal'. It is easy to let the stirrups down as you relax. If you start with them over-long you may look loose and insecure in your riding.

- The stirrup leathers should lie flat along your leg. (Element 3.3.1) If you inadvertently have a turn in the leather, then the edge of the stirrup leather will lie against your leg, and usually feels uncomfortable. The spare length of stirrup

Correct holding of the reins. Hands level, and thumbs uppermost with wrists relaxed.

leather should stay behind your thigh so that it does not pinch you. It does not have to be put through the keeper as long as it stays back.

- Pick up the reins smoothly and with feel. The reins should be held one in each hand, with the hands level; the thumbs should be on the top of the rein with the fingers closed around the rein; the wrists and elbows should be relaxed, and there should be an imaginary line from the elbow, through the forearm, through the rein to the horse's mouth, so that an even contact is sustained on the reins. (Element 3.4.1) There should be no twists in the reins, and the spare length of rein should be below the reins, not resting over the top of them, which would send the weight of the reins down to the horse's mouth.

Show:

The correct basics in the ability to maintain a correct, balanced position when riding with stirrups.

ELEMENT

| C | **4.1.1** Show a correct, secure and balanced position at walk with stirrups at a suitable length for riding on the flat. |

| C | **4.2.1** Show a correct, secure and balanced position at trot with stirrups at a suitable length for riding on the flat. |

| S | **4.3.1** Show a correct, secure and balanced position at canter with stirrups at a suitable length for riding on the flat. |

What the assessor will look for

- The correct basics **MUST** be seen. (Elements 4.1.1, 4.2.1 and 4.3.1) The basic balanced position – the rider sitting centrally in the saddle, the weight evenly on both seat bones, an imaginary straight line running ear–shoulder–hip–heel, the

The correct position for the rider, as seen from the side. Notice the shoulder–hip–heel alignment.

rider demonstrating balance over the lower leg from a secure seat – is essential. The hand position already described adds a dimension of balance and harmony in that the rider is 'with' the horse and able to follow the basic movements and influence the horse's pace and direction.

- Work to develop the basic riding position on the flat: it is the foundation of your riding future. The more smoothly you can move from one pace to another whilst sustaining balance and position, the better.

Show:

The correct basics in the ability to maintain a correct, balanced position when riding without stirrups.

ELEMENT

C **5.1.1** Show a correct, secure and balanced position at walk without stirrups.

C **5.2.1** Show a correct, secure and balanced position at trot without stirrups.

What the assessor will look for

- The whole development of your riding is based on your basic position and balance. This enables you to control and influence your horse safely and effectively.

- Moving from one pace to another will constantly demonstrate your balance and co-ordination, which must be secure and harmonious.

- There is a need for you to look in harmony with the horse, and your ability to 'feel' how the horse is reacting to you must become an intrinsic part of your riding.

- Gripping up with the lower leg without stirrups, particularly in trot, is a common indicator that your balance is not well established and that you then rely on tightening the lower leg to stay on the horse. Aim to develop your suppleness and relaxation so that you can continually let your legs relax and lengthen around the horse. Try to work to open your leg up and back at the hip and soften your thigh.

- Maintain a straight position in the saddle, be careful not to tip inwards or allow your seat to slip to one side of the saddle. Your regular teacher should work with you to ensure that you are consistently sitting straight in the saddle. Crookedness will eventually have an adverse effect on the horse and will inhibit your ability to develop your riding with level influence.

- Make sure that you feel very confident about working without stirrups in walk and trot. Although you will not be asked to canter without stirrups in your exam, it is well worth your while being able to do so. Then when you are required to demonstrate only walk and trot, you will be working well within your level of competence. You will ride for up to 10 minutes without your stirrups and must feel confident about this.

Show:

The correct basics in the ability to maintain a correct, balanced position in preparation for jumping.

ELEMENT

| C | **6.1.1** Maintain a correct, secure and balanced position at the trot in the jumping seat with stirrups at a suitable length. |

| S | **6.2.1** Maintain a correct, secure and balanced position at the canter in the jumping seat with stirrups at a suitable length. |

What the assessor will look for

- You need to feel equally confident about riding at your 'normal flat length' and at 'jumping position length'. You must develop the ability to move from jumping position to upright position and back again, with no loss of balance to yourself and no loss of harmony or rhythm in the horse.

- Adopt a stirrup length shorter than your 'flat' length, and from this be able to demonstrate a balance of your body weight distributed between the lower leg and the lighter seat. The angles between the lower leg and knee, and the thigh and upper body, are more closed as the rider takes the upper body a little forward, while still securely supported over the lower leg. The seat moves a little back in the saddle and the rider adopts a shorter rein length with the reins either

Light seat/jumping position. You must ride in balance. At faster paces, e.g. galloping across country, the upper body may be more forward than in a basic light seat/jumping position.

side of the horse's neck. The rider looks up and the back is flat with the shoulders back. The seat is neither raised out of the saddle nor sitting down, as it is in the dressage seat position.

- You must feel confident to adopt the light seat/jumping position in walk, trot and canter around the school, either as an individual exercise or in open order. (Elements 6.1.1 and 6.2.1)

Light seat/jumping position, with the rider's weight absorbed through the lower leg, and the seat just 'breathing' on the saddle. (This rider may be using her hands a little to help her balance, which is incorrect.)

Standing up in the stirrups – an exercise to help riders find balance over their lower leg security.

- Learn to 'stand up in your stirrups' as this is an exercise which helps you develop balance and security in the light seat/jumping position.

Show:

The correct basics in the ability to maintain a correct, balanced position when working over poles.

ELEMENT

C   **7.1.1** Demonstrate a correct, secure, and balanced position at the trot in the light, balanced jumping seat with stirrups at a suitable length over ground poles.

What the assessor will look for

- You will be required to trot over trotting poles, either on the long side of the arena or on one or both diagonal lines of the school. You must be able to:

*Trotting over poles – the rider showing a balanced light
seat/jumping position and a straight line through the poles.*

1. Ride a good corner and maintain a good line of approach to the poles.

2. Adopt a good, balanced light seat/jumping position just before the poles and maintain it through the poles and for a stride or two away.

3. Ride a good, straight line of departure away from the poles to a well-ridden corner and back onto the outside track.

4. Control the speed and activity of the horse so that he can maintain a clear rhythm through the poles.

5. Demonstrate an independent position that is never reliant on the reins for balance.

6. Demonstrate suppleness and good balance in harmony with the horse.

7. Maintain distances or ride independently to the poles as required.

Show:

A basic understanding of the natural aids.

ELEMENT

| C | **8.1.1** Demonstrate the natural aids for riding the horse forward correctly. |

| S | **8.2.1** Demonstrate the natural aids for riding correct circles. |

| S | **8.3.1** Demonstrate the natural aids for riding correct turns. |

| S | **8.4.1** Demonstrate the natural aids for riding correct straight lines. |

SCHOOL FIGURES

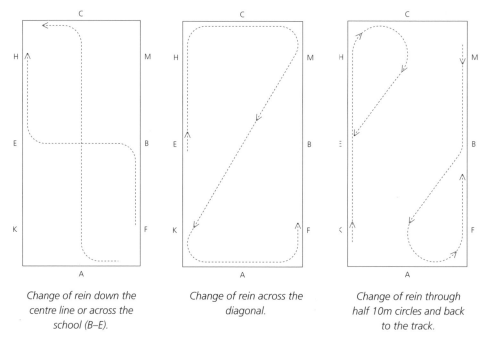

Change of rein down the centre line or across the school (B–E).

Change of rein across the diagonal.

Change of rein through half 10m circles and back to the track.

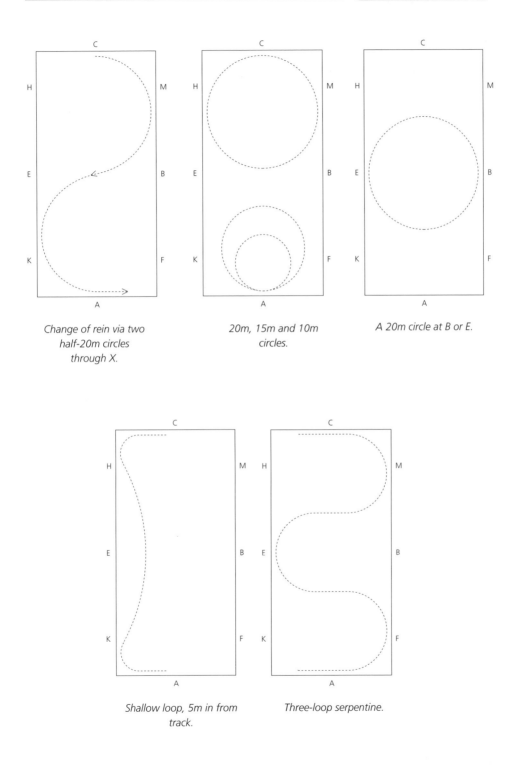

Change of rein via two
half-20m circles
through X.

20m, 15m and 10m
circles.

A 20m circle at B or E.

Shallow loop, 5m in from
track.

Three-loop serpentine.

What the assessor will look for

- Be very clear in your own mind about the basic aids for control. Very simply:

  - The rider's inside leg sends the horse forward and creates impulsion; it motivates the horse's inside hind leg and assists in helping the horse to be flexible on turns, circles and any line which is not straight.

  - The rider's outside leg, usually slightly further back than the 'on the girth' position of the inside leg, also assists in forward movement, but specifically controls the hindquarters and prevents them from swinging out, encouraging them to 'follow' the front legs on turns and circles.

  - The rider's inside hand creates a slight flexion in the horse's head and neck (gullet) but never greater than the bend through the rest of the body.

  - The rider's outside hand controls the speed of the pace and also regulates the bend created by the inside rein.

- You must clearly demonstrate an ability to use these basic aids to produce independent forward movement (not just following another horse) on straight lines, turns and circles. (Elements 8.1.1, 8.2.1, 8.3.1 and 8.4.1)

- You must be able to ride accurate and active turns and circles (20m).

- You must be able to ride forward to halt and maintain immobility in halt.

- All this work must show not only that you have the ability to influence the horse effectively through basic figures, but also that your position is sufficiently secure and established to be able to ride the horse and movements without any dependence on the reins to maintain your balance. (Elements 4 and 5)

Practise riding turns and circles in many different situations in the school. Think of how many different places you can ride a 20m circle and practise it in walk, trot and canter, with and without your stirrups and in rising and sitting trot. Practise riding turns and inclines across the school, sometimes changing the rein through a turn and sometimes staying on the same rein. Practise all this work in closed order in a ride and also in open order.

Know:

The reasons for trotting on named diagonals.

ELEMENT

 9.1.1 Demonstrate an ability to rise with correct diagonals.

What the assessor will look for

- You must be entirely familiar with the concept of diagonals in trot, their use and their value to you and the horse.

- Diagonals exist in trot because the trot pace is two-time and the legs move in diagonal pairs.

- The diagonals are named from the front legs (left diagonal is the left foreleg with the right hind leg; the right diagonal is the right foreleg with the left hind leg).

- It is in the interests of the balance and suppleness of both horse and rider to ride on both diagonals in rising trot, so that the work is even on both reins.

the rider's seat comes out of the saddle as the horse's left shoulder goes forward

the rider's seat returns to the saddle as the horse's left shoulder comes back

Riding on a specific diagonal in trot. Here the rider is on the left diagonal.

- It is usual to ride on the outside diagonal, i.e. to sit in the saddle as the outside diagonal is on the ground. (On the left rein this means you sit on the right diagonal, and on the right rein you sit on the left diagonal.)

- For simplicity it is easier to refer to the 'inside' and 'outside' diagonal rather than the left and right diagonal. Confusion can arise if you are on the right rein and an instructor tells you that you are on the 'right' diagonal (meaning the correct or outside diagonal) when you think you are on the left diagonal (which is in fact the one you are on!).

- Become familiar with changing the diagonal by sitting for one extra beat (step). Maintain your balance; do not collapse your back and sit heavily.

- Become familiar with knowing which diagonal you are on. First, glance at the horse's shoulders and decide which shoulder is coming back as you are sitting in the saddle. When the shoulder comes back, the same foot is on the floor; when the shoulder moves forward, the foot is in the air.

- Eventually you will develop feel for which diagonal you are on, but this takes time and practice. Some horses give you a clearer 'feel' than others. If in doubt, check by glancing down – do this with your eyes only. Do not allow your whole upper body to be affected by leaning forward.

- Get into the habit of occasionally checking your diagonal just to be sure you are on the correct one.

- If you are in rising trot remember to change diagonal every time you change direction, e.g. in changes of rein, in serpentine loops and on any occasion when there is a sustained change of the horse's bend.

- The occasional incorrect diagonal during your exam will not cause you to 'fail'. Only if you show a total lack of awareness or understanding of the use of diagonals on both the horses that you ride, is this likely to be considered an area which is not up to the standard required by a Stage 1 rider.

Know:

An incorrect leading leg in canter, and trot to enable a correct lead to be established.

ELEMENT

C **10.1.1** Demonstrate an ability to recognise cantering with the correct leading leg.

C **10.1.2** Use corners/half circles to help ensure correct strike-offs into canter.

What the assessor will look for

- Understanding the reason why horses canter on a 'leading leg' is essential at this level. You must feel very familiar with the fact that:

  - In canter the horse's legs move in three-time.

  - The sequence of the horse's legs in canter is:

    outside hind leg forms the first beat,

    outside foreleg with the inside hind leg forms the second beat,

    inside foreleg forms the third beat,

    and then there is a moment of suspension when all four legs are off the ground at the same time.

- Naturally the horse is likely to give this sequence of legs whenever he canters unhindered and in balance, particularly on a curved line.

- We call the third beat of the canter the 'leading leg' because it appears to strike out in advance of the outside foreleg and 'lead' the canter.

- Remember, the way you apply the aids for a canter transition will help the horse to strike off on the correct leading leg.

- Ensure that the horse is in a balanced active trot before asking for canter.

- Ask for canter in a corner or on a half circle as this will encourage the horse to offer the correct lead. Often the first corner of the short side of the school is the better one to choose as the horse still has another corner to go round to encourage him to strike off correctly.

- Apply your inside leg on the girth, your outside leg behind the girth, while maintaining the bend with the inside rein and controlling the pace with the outside rein.

- Try to develop 'feel' for the horse giving you the correct lead in canter. If he strikes off on the 'wrong' leg, try to feel the discomfort to you as the rider and the lack of balance that the horse is demonstrating.

- If you 'look' for the leading leg, make quite sure that you only use your eyes – taking the body forward to look often unbalances the horse further and may actually encourage him to strike off on the wrong leg. (Elements 10.1.1 and 10.1.2)

An incorrect canter lead will not cause you to 'fail' your Stage 1 exam. Several incorrect leads, of which you appear to have no awareness, coupled with poor preparation for canter transitions and no correction of the fault when it occurs, are more likely to contribute to the assessor deciding that your competence is not yet sufficient for Stage 1.

Know:

How to handle the reins.

ELEMENT

S   **11.1.1** Show a correctly maintained rein contact throughout.

Changing the whip. Take the reins into one hand (the hand holding the whip),
use the free hand to take the whip smoothly over the wither (as shown),
then re-take both reins.

What the assessor will look for

- This element covers an overall observation of you as a rider. You should aim to maintain a consistent and 'feeling' contact with the horse through the rein in all your work. At no time should the rein be in loops (unless you are walking on a loose rein!) with no connection to the horse's mouth; conversely the rein should not be over-short and demonstrate tension and restriction, to which the horse is likely to show resistance.

- Your aim is to become a feeling rider with security in your position so that your balance is independent of the reins at all times. You can then work to develop a fluent, communicative, active rein contact throughout all your work.

- Work on your basic position. It is from a depth of seat and independence that a consistent rein contact is established.

- Your hands should always 'think' forwards and have that light but firm feel, as if you are holding a small bird comfortably in your hands.

Know:

How to handle a whip.

ELEMENT

S **12.1.1** Demonstrate correct use of a whip which does not exceed 75cm (30ins).

What the assessor will look for

- In holding and using a whip you must always show co-ordination and judgement.

- Handling of the whip while mounting, and in your basic riding, will be observed. At no time should the whip inconvenience you or the horse. You must learn to handle it carefully and efficiently when mounting and dismounting.

- When mounting, hold the whip in your left hand. If somebody is giving you a leg-up then put the whip to the offside, down the horse's shoulder. If the stirrup is being held down for you on the offside then leave the whip on the near side, down the horse's shoulder. If you are mounting unaided then it does not matter which shoulder you hold the whip against.

- When dismounting, always put the whip in your left hand, down the horse's left shoulder.

- You must learn to change the whip over smoothly by taking the reins into one hand when you change the direction. The whip should usually be carried in your inside hand where it supports the inside leg.

- If the horse is lazy to your leg or ignores your leg, the reins should be taken in one hand and the whip used smartly behind your inside leg on the horse's flank. There should be a reaction; the whip should not be used repeatedly in an aimless way because your leg does not have sufficient effect.

- Part of the exam is to assess your judgment as to whether or not you need to use the whip. If you need to use it then you should do so.

Questions and Answers

The following are a sample of the questions, along with suggested answers, which are regularly used in BHS exams by assessors.

Horse Behaviour

Q. What is the horse's natural lifestyle?

A. Herd animal. Constantly browsing and grazing. Living in a group of other horses, where a 'pecking order' is likely to develop.

Q. Name some instincts of the horse.

A. To survive, usually by flight (runs away from something fearful). Feeding. Breeding. Sixth sense, which creates a reaction for which there appears to be no cause.

Q. What is the horse's natural reaction if frightened:
  (a) In the field?
  (b) In the stable?
  (c) When ridden?

A. (a) Runs away in a group and then stands at the end of the field looking back with head up and nostrils flared, maybe snorting.

A. (b) Head into the corner, bottom to the perceived danger.

A. (c) May buck, could rear; could try to run away from or spook at the perceived object of fear.

Q. What is likely to upset him?

A. Sudden noises or unexpected activity, particularly if he cannot see where the noise is coming from.

The Horse at Grass

Q. What is the normal behaviour in the field?

A. Horses grazing, usually in a group; some horses may be resting under a tree or just browsing in the sunshine. If cold and windy then horses tend to huddle together for communal shelter; they will turn their backs into the wind and weather. If content and secure then horses may lie down in the sun on a warm day.

Q. What sort of behaviour in the field would lead you to take a closer look at the horses?

A. One horse standing away from the group, either looking dejected or ostracised. One horse behaving differently or abnormally from the rest. All the horses running around looking anxious or harassed.

Q. What sort of behaviour can cause problems with groups of horses living together?

A. Sometimes geldings get possessive and fight each other if there is a mare in the group, particularly if she comes into season. If there is a dominant male horse he may threaten or bully other horses in the group causing them distress or anxiety. Generally, entire horses (stallions) or rigs (horses which have not been completely or successfully castrated) should not be kept in the same field as geldings, and certainly not with mares.

Q. How would you expect a horse to behave when turned out after a long period of being stabled? When turning him out, why must you be careful?

A. He is likely to be highly excited, wanting to gallop about in the wide open space and then eventually to eat grass voraciously. When turning him out it would be wise to try to put him with a companion who is older and calm (and who has been out regularly) so that his desire to gallop is not encouraged by another horse behaving in the same way. Try to turn him out on a warm, sunny, quiet day when he is more likely to settle and eat, rather than a cold, windy day which is more likely to have him running about to keep warm. Try to turn him out when he is a bit hungry (just before a meal) so that he is more inclined to want to eat than to run.

Q. Some horses are difficult to catch. Why do you think this happens, and how can you use the horse's natural instincts to overcome this problem?

A. The horse may associate being caught with working and he may be reluctant to come in to work. He may enjoy his freedom and not wish to be stabled. He may want to stay with his friends, if you are trying to remove him from his companions. You can overcome this problem by catching all the other horses in the field first, so that the difficult-to-catch horse thinks he is going to be left on his own. Take the other horses to the gate as if to bring them out of the field. Tempt the difficult horse with food and then feed him when you bring him in, so that he associates coming in with food (before he has to work). Sometimes catch him, feed him and turn him out again, so that he does not always associate coming in with being worked.

Q. How might a horse, used to living out, behave in a strange field with a strange companion?

A. The horse may run around the perimeter of the field, literally examining the boundaries. He may sniff and squeal at his new companion; they may strike out at each other and then run around before hopefully settling to graze in close proximity to each other. If they do not settle, you may need to watch out for one horse harassing or bullying the other; in this case they may need to be separated.

Q. How might a horse behave if you separate him from his favourite companion by putting them in different fields?

A. He may be anxious and unsettled, running up and down the fence line or by the gate, calling to his friend. If the other horse is in earshot they may call to each other. In rarer circumstances one horse may try to jump out to rejoin his friend.

Q. How might a horse behave if you turn him out in a field on his own?

A. Some horses are used to going out alone and will be quite content. However, a horse used to company may be anxious; he will stay by the gate, pace up and down the fence, threaten to jump out and call and shout to anyone who may listen or answer him.

Q. You catch a horse and leave his companion alone in the field. How might the latter behave?

A. He may show signs of stressful behaviour and anxiety, as described in the preceding question.

Q. When releasing a horse into a field, what sort of behaviour might occur which would endanger you?

A. Turning horses out can be potentially dangerous for the handler. If a horse is excitable and anxious to get out to grass, he may try to dash off before you have completely released the headcollar. In this case you could receive a nasty wrench or pull on your fingers or arms. You should always turn the horse back towards the gate before letting him go, as then he must turn around before running away and this gives you a moment to move out of range. Horses often kick up their heels as they run off to play or eat, and it is very easy to receive a nasty kick from the heels of a disappearing horse.

Q. When releasing horses into a field, how might other horses behave if one horse is let go and gallops off?

A. If releasing more than one horse then there must be a signal between handlers to ensure that all horses are released at the same time. This minimises the risk of one horse charging off and the others trying to follow before the handlers are ready. If one horse is turned out into a field where other horses are already grazing, then the occupants may stop grazing and run up to the newcomer. They may then all run off together. As the handler, be ready to release the horse as quickly and efficiently as possible, and then stay out of the way of any approaching loose horses.

Q. It has been a cold, wet night. The horse is cold and miserable. How will it behave?

A. He will look dejected, head down, and huddled, perhaps against a hedge or fence line, trying to stay out of the wind. His coat will be wet and heavy, although if he has sufficient coat he should still be dry underneath the top, wet layer. He may be standing away from the rest of the group and will probably be keen to come in when you come to catch him. If very cold he may shiver visibly.

Q. Do horses lie down in the field? Is it a good sign when they do?

A. When horses are content and secure in their environment, and the weather is warm and sunny, then horses sometimes lie down. However, if a horse is lying down in inclement weather then this would not be a good sign.

The Horse in the Stable

Q. Why should you always speak to your horse before handling him?

A. So that the horse is aware of your presence and you do not take him by surprise, which might cause him to react instinctively (kick out or try to run away).

Q. Before touching a hind leg or foot, why should you pat the horse and run your hand along his body and down over his quarters?

A. The horse is then aware of where you are and which part of his body you are aiming for. If you touched a hind leg without any warning, the horse could react instinctively and kick out at you.

Q. What do the horse's ears tell you?

A. The ears indicate the horse's confidence and state of mind. If the horse is anxious his ears will be half turned back and look tense; if confident and happy, his ears will be forward and relaxed; if interested or alert, his ears will be pointed sharply forward. An angry or unhappy horse flattens his ears back against his head and looks miserable and bad-tempered.

Q. What do you have to be aware of when first working in the stable, or when grooming a strange horse?

A. The horse should always be tied up for his own and your safety. Be aware of the attitude of the horse: how confident he seems, how relaxed and happy he is – watch his body language and his ears. Move carefully and sympathetically around him at all times. Always let him know where you are and what you are about to do.

Q. A new horse comes into the yard. How might he behave if he has never been stabled before?

A. He may be anxious in the stable. He may rush to the door and look unsettled; he will not relax and be calm. Giving him a haynet may encourage him to settle and eat, as will putting him next door to another horse that he can see behaving in a calm, relaxed manner.

Q. If a horse is worried by new surroundings, what would be the signs?

A. The horse would look restless and unsettled. He may frequently pass small amounts of droppings. He may rush to the stable door, look out then pace around the stable. He won't settle and eat. His whole demeanour and body language is one of tension and anxiety.

Q.When you first handle a horse, what signs would tell you he was easy to handle?

A. He would be calm, relaxed and confident with you. His ears would be relaxed and happy; likewise his stance or movement in the stable would be relaxed. He would stand quietly while tied up, move over and pick up his feet with ease and without fuss. He would be quiet and enjoyable to work with.

Q. A horse is described as quiet to handle in the stable. How should he behave?

A. See the answer to the previous question. All these criteria apply.

Q. If a horse is inclined to bite, what precautions should you take before handling him or when adjusting his rugs?

A. Always tie up the horse before doing anything with him. If necessary, tie him quite short, or 'cross tie' him, i.e. attach a rope to each side of his headcollar so he cannot bite you from either side. Everyone involved in handling this horse should know about his bad habit, and only people competent in dealing with the fault should handle him.

Q. Do horses lie down in the stable? Is it a good sign if they do?

A. Some horses do lie down, particularly at night. The same criteria apply to the question of the horse lying down in the field. If the horse is secure and content he may lie down, and this demonstrates confidence. Unusual lying down, or lying down and showing signs of discomfort or pain, would cause concern.

The Horse when Ridden

Q. What sort of things affect a horse's behaviour when being ridden?

A. He may be upset by unfamiliar or sudden noises, particularly if he cannot see the source of the sound, e.g. a lawnmower. He may be frightened by black bin bags left out for the dustman. He may be less confident and more spooky if he is on his own. If riding outside in wind and rain he may be reluctant to 'face' into the bad weather.

Q. What type of horse do you consider suitable for a novice rider? How important is temperament?

A. A horse of some maturity and experience (not a very young, 'green' horse). A calm horse, and usually a half-bred horse or a 'cold-blooded' horse, not usually a thoroughbred. A horse with smooth, comfortable paces who reacts steadily and not suddenly or unpredictably. Temperament is very important. A calm, equable, amenable horse is ideal.

Q. We talk about horses having (a) a good temperament and (b) a nervous temperament. What do we mean?

A. (a) A good temperament is one where the horse is calm, predictable, pleasant to be around and to handle. He is tolerant of everything and nothing seems to bother him. He is biddable and amenable in every respect.

A. (b) A nervous temperament is one where the horse demonstrates anxiety and uncertainty in his behaviour. He is unpredictable and easily upset by the least change in circumstances. He is not calm or reliable.

Q. How would a horse show he was feeling fresh when he is first mounted?

A. He might not stand still and quietly while being mounted. He might become tight through his back and feel tense to the rider. He might try to rush off rather than wait for the rider's instruction. He might even try and put his head down and buck.

Q. What is a fresh horse?

A. A fresh horse is one who is feeling very full of himself. He may have been fed too much for the amount of work he is doing. He may have been shut in the stable and not turned out/worked hard for a day or two. He may just be feeling very well and on a bright spring day or a cold winter's day he just comes out feeling rather cheerful.

Q. How can you tell your horse is afraid of an object on the side of the road?

A. He will 'spook' at the object, trying to avoid going near it; he may try to run past it quickly because he is frightened of it. He may refuse to pass it, trying to turn around and go back the way he has come.

Q. How might your horse warn you that he is not happy about another horse approaching him in the ride?

A. He might lay his ears back and look angrily at the approaching horse. If the horse comes too close, he may turn his bottom towards it in a threatening gesture, or he may try to bite it. If it comes up behind him, your horse may stop abruptly and try to back up to the approaching horse and possibly kick out.

Q. What are the horse's natural defences when attacked?

A. To run away. To strike out at the danger with the hind feet, or, if necessary, with the front feet. To rear and swing around to avoid the attacker. If the 'attacker' is on his back then he would buck and plunge.

Taking the Exam

Assessors are professional instructors with many years' experience of training students and examining the standards they are aiming for. There will be a chief assessor, and probably two or three other assessors. They should all introduce themselves at the beginning of the day and they should wear a badge with their name on so that you can identify them. They are truly **human** and they like nothing better than to pass **everyone**. However, there is a standard to maintain and that is their responsibility. If you are up to standard **you will pass**. Assessors should smile and put you at your ease. They are **not** there to make the day traumatic for you; they are there to help you to do your best.

Exam psychology

You **must** go into the exam believing in yourself and in the competence you have achieved. If you have worked hard and have covered every aspect of the work required by the syllabus; if you can answer all the questions relative to the work at this level and can ride in a balanced co-ordinated way on sensible, trained horses; if you feel familiar with handling horses in the stable, carrying out the basic tasks required of this standard, then all you have to do on the day is go and show the assessors how competent you are.

Ultimately only you can dispel the nerves which inevitably will be there before you start. Do not allow nerves to fail you. You must learn to control them. Once you start the actual exam and have something to do, concentrate on the tasks and on showing your ability.

If you think you have made a mistake (and often you think that something is a major fault whereas the assessors think it a very minor fault!), put it behind you and think positively. Don't be so busy thinking about the error that you allow it to cloud the rest of the exam. Take the attitude that it will be the **only** fault you show, not the first of many. If you have trained hard enough then **you** (yes, **you**) have the capacity to pass. Go in and show the assessors how good you are.

Exam procedure

- The Stage 1 exam will take half a day. There will usually be up to eighteen candidates.

- You will be divided into three groups for the whole exam. Sometimes there are a few candidates taking just the riding section or the care section on its own. In this case they will join one of the groups for the section of the exam they are covering.

- The riding exam will usually take place in an indoor school, but in the summer, if the weather is good, it could be held on an outdoor surface. It will always be in a marked arena.

- You will ride two horses in the exam and this will give you the opportunity to demonstrate your competence equally on both horses. You may 'like' one horse better than the other, but do not allow this to inhibit you from riding competently at the level required.

- On the first horse you will ride in your basic riding position, with stirrups at the length that you feel appropriate for work on the flat. At some time on the second horse you will be asked to take up your stirrups and demonstrate the light seat/jumping position in preparation for jumping.

- A member of staff from the riding centre will 'command' the ridden section. The caller/commander is there to help you do your best. If you need help or don't understand at any stage, then say so and ask for the instruction to be repeated.

- The stable management testing will be covered in two or three sections.

- All the practical tasks will be carried out in the stable yard.

- You will work either individually with one horse per candidate or with another candidate sharing the same horse.

- If working alone, select the equipment you need and take it to the stable. If you need to leave the stable, for example to change something, always make sure that the horse is tied up and the stable door closed. Never leave the horse with equipment half on (e.g. don't leave the saddle on while going to fetch a girth!).

STAGE 1 PROGRAMME

Maximum 18 Candidates

*All sections include 10 mins at the end to complete paperwork, if preferred the programme can be adjusted by Chief and completed at end of exam.

8.30   **BRIEFING**

	Ride and part practical oral	Practical	Theory and part practical oral
9.00-10.15	Group A	Group B	Group C
10.25-11.40	Group B	Group C	Group A
11.50-1.05	Group C	Group A	Group B
1.05	EXAM ENDS (approx)		

Typical examination timetable.

- If working with another candidate, always complete your own task so that you can talk about what you have done – for example, you put on the saddle, and the other person puts on the bridle.

- There will be a separate section where tasks such as standing the horse for inspection, mucking out, carrying weights, tying haynets, etc. are covered. This section will be attended by the whole group, with individuals being asked to carry out tasks while there is some communal discussion about the procedures.

- Make sure that you volunteer information whenever you can. Don't wait to be asked a question if there is an opportunity to show your knowledge without interrupting others.

- The assessor should control the group so that you all have the opportunity to input on each subject.

- The stable management theory section will cover all the subjects which are not covered by the practical work or which do not lend themselves to practical demonstration. These could include feeding, grassland and subjects such as the horse's behaviour when ridden and in the stable.

- The assessor should control the group, asking individuals to answer questions. Do take the opportunity to add information where you can, and if someone says something that you disagree with, be prepared to ask the assessor if you can add to what has been said and then politely state your opinion.

- Try to be clear and forthcoming in your discussion sections. Practise putting the information across in a clear, factual way which demonstrates your knowledge and does not waste time in 'waffle' without divulging any facts.

The next step and how to access it

If you are in a formal training situation (in a college or a training yard) you will probably receive plenty of guidance from your tutors or instructors as to how to proceed with your studies towards Stage 2. If you are working on BHS exams on your own, or perhaps receiving day-release training on a weekly or monthly basis, while working full-time in the horse industry, you may not be so clear as to how to progress towards Stage 2.

When you achieve any level of competence, then you must practise at that level, to consolidate the expertise, and not be in too much of a hurry to immediately aim for the next Stage. Have a long-term goal for achieving Stage 2 but allow yourself a little 'space' to enjoy your achievement at Stage 1 before loading yourself with further study. If you are working in the industry, then hopefully your practical day-to-day work will consolidate your competence and gradually you can study the requirements of the next level, beginning to plan how you will achieve the added expertise both in your riding and stable management skills.

Stage 2 will further challenge your riding ability and require that you are proficient in basic jumping. Stage 2 stable management will require that you are capable of looking after stabled horses or those kept at grass with a minimum of supervision for the basic, day-to-day requirements of those horses. The Stage exams are designed to allow you to progress smoothly from one level to another, ensuring that a thorough amount of hands-on practical experience is coupled with the theoretical knowledge.

Further Reading

The following books and booklets can all be obtained from the BHS Bookshop.

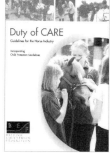

Guide to BHS Examinations

Examinations Handbook

BHS Guide to Careers with Horses

Duty of Care

Useful Addresses

British Horse Society
Stoneleigh Deer Park
Kenilworth
Warwickshire
CV8 2XZ
tel: 08701 202244 or 01926 707700
fax: 01926 707800
website: www.bhs.org.uk
email: enquiry@bhs.org.uk

BHS Examinations Department
(address as above)
tel: 01926 707784
fax: 01926 707792
email: exams@bhs.org.uk

BHS Training Department
(address as above)
tel: 01926 707820
    01926 707799
email: training@bhs.org.uk

**BHS Riding Schools/Approvals
    Department**
(address as above)
tel: 01926 707795
fax: 01926 707796
email: Riding.Schools@bhs.org.uk

BHS Bookshop
(address as above)
tel: 08701 201918
    01926 707762
website: www.britishhorse.com

The BHS Examination System

Outline of progression route through
BHS examinations

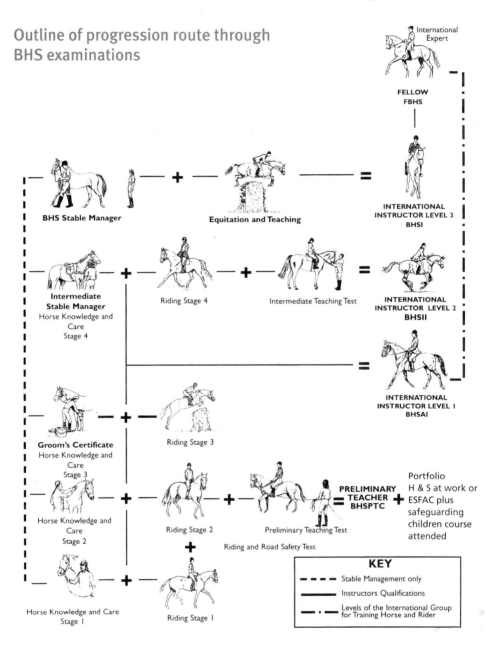

International
Expert

**FELLOW
FBHS**

**INTERNATIONAL
INSTRUCTOR LEVEL 3
BHSI**

BHS Stable Manager

Equitation and Teaching

**Intermediate
Stable Manager**
Horse Knowledge and
Care
Stage 4

Riding Stage 4

Intermediate Teaching Test

**INTERNATIONAL
INSTRUCTOR LEVEL 2
BHSII**

**INTERNATIONAL
INSTRUCTOR LEVEL I
BHSAI**

Groom's Certificate
Horse Knowledge and
Care
Stage 3

Riding Stage 3

Horse Knowledge and
Care
Stage 2

Riding Stage 2

Preliminary Teaching Test

Riding and Road Safety Test

**PRELIMINARY
TEACHER
BHSPTC**

Portfolio
H & S at work or
ESFAC plus
safeguarding
children course
attended

Horse Knowledge and Care
Stage I

Riding Stage I

KEY

– – – Stable Management only

——— Instructors Qualifications

—·— Levels of the International Group
for Training Horse and Rider